The Best Self-Help Book Ever Written

Julianne Soviero

Copyright © 2018 Julianne Soviero
All rights reserved.
ISBN: 978-0-9995502-0-5

ACKNOWLEDGEMENTS

There are so many people who have been instrumental in my writing career and my business career. I never ever could have done all of this alone.

Massive thanks to my husband, who somehow believes that I am capable of doing anything. His unwavering belief in me is undoubtedly the reason why I was Valedictorian, opened my own business, have written four books, and am now carrying our beautiful son. Life is so much better when someone believes in you.

Massive thanks to my parents, who gave me the love and the life lessons I needed to be successful.

Vito Lafata, I know that you were kind of against me writing this book, but I am going to thank you anyway. Not only because you are an amazing business coach, but also because you have ignited in me a fire for personal development that I didn't even know existed.

Rob Crews: what would I do without you constantly getting me even MORE excited about my life than usual? I have all I can do to keep up with you sometimes.

Thank you to my amazing clients: so many of our conversations have inspired different parts of this book. Most importantly, I hope that this book really helps you where you need help and lets you know how to take control of your life.

Thank you to Melanie Rushing: having a success partner is awesome. You are amazing girl!

Also, thank you to Chris Hemsworth and the Twilight Vampires for making it so that I can be kind of funny at times. Finally, thank you to *Fifty Shades of Grey*, for making the literary bar so low that this book will look like it was written by a genius.

CONTENTS

	Introduction	i
1	Organization: You're Welcome	1
2	Gooooaaaalllllllllls!!!!!!!!!	26
3	Where All Your Damn Money is Going	32
4	Wait, I'm Supposed to be Nice?	45
5	Why it's So Easy to Be Fat and Sick	57
6	Spoiler Alert: Energy Actually Doesn't Come in a Cup	70
7	Kaizen	81
8	Gratitude	87
9	Motivation	92
10	Your Comfort Zone and Why It Sucks	98

INTRODUCTION

Are you tired of those twenty-page introductions in which someone goes on and on using not-so-subtle name-dropping to highlight all of the high-end clients and celebrities that the author has worked with? I feel like I can barely get through a page of most of these books without seeing "Oprah" or some other really recognizable name that would make you think, "wow, if the author worked with THAT person, then the author must really know his shit."

Well, you will find none of that self-aggrandizement here: mainly because I have never worked with Oprah. If I had, you would never hear the end of it. I would be like, "my best friend Oprah: Oprah, Oprah, Oprah." So even though I haven't *yet* worked with Oprah ("stalking" is not the same as "working with" right? Just checking), I have a bunch of other credentials. Mainly, I have helped lots and lots of people just like you. That's right: NOT people like Oprah who can essentially pay someone to manage every element of their lives for them, but normal people who just want to make their lives a little better. I am also at a place where I know how to manage finances in a way that I think is pretty impressive given that I have no financial background and had to take on a ton of debt that was not my own. I am at a really good place for being only 37 years old AND none of this is magic or rocket science. I am not one of these coaches who has a team of highly paid advisors telling me how to make my life great. I just READ. I am a person who loves what she does, has set up her financial future, has good relationships, and has created her dream job.

I mean, that's pretty sweet, but it is also very accessible. I want you to realize that we are essentially the same, but I have read about a million self-help books, done crazy continuing education, and have filtered through all of the crap to only bring you the best and most important stuff. In case you want more, though, I am also going to refer you to several great books throughout this book that will allow you to dive deeper into certain subject areas. These books, in my opinion, are the best of the best, and give you instructions on how to take action steps to make your life better every day.

So get ready. We are going to dig deep, but we are also going to have fun. This is it: *The Best Self-Help Book Ever Written*

1 ORGANIZATION: YOU'RE WELCOME

Are my husband and I the only ones who read personal development books and feel like the first thirty pages are all filler and nonsense? It's like, okay, I get it, Julia Roberts' life would be a mess without the advice of this amazing coach whose book I am currently reading: duly noted. This led me to some existential pensiveness. I thought, everyone is always bragging about working with celebrities, but celebrities often have failed marriages (plural), yo-yoing weight, insane debt, substance abuse problems, and all sorts of other problems that I have fortunately never had to deal with. I mean, does that sound so great? I would prefer the life I have built for myself, thank you very much.

Some of you are all-too-familiar with the latest celebrity drama because you have a penchant for reading about them or doing the click bait thing. This can seem kind of harmless at first, but celebrity gossip is a waste of time at best, and an impediment to your dreams at worst. The time that you spend reading about Taylor Swift's latest romantic plane crash can be time you spend developing yourself or creating your ideal life. Really! You can create a better life in just a few minutes a day.

Here is a news flash: wasting time is: The. Worst. Thing. Ever!

Why?
1. You, as a mere mortal (unless you are a vampire or other undead creature, in which case, you will have a completely different set of problems), only have a very finite amount of time to make an impact on this planet. So when other people

waste your time or (maybe worse) you waste your own time, value is ultimately being detracted from your life
2. Everything out there is a time trap! We should have more free time now that everything is so accessible and at our fingertips, but instead we spend hours mindlessly browsing or hours mindlessly watching tv, and that is a minor tragedy.

When you were little, and people asked you what you wanted to be when you grew up, you probably didn't say, "I would like a mediocre job that I will hate. Oh, and coming home from said job will necessitate several hours of numbing my brain in front of the television."

I mean, did you say that? Because if you did, this book is probably not for you. Nope, you are exactly where you want to be right now.

Take some time to really connect with yourself. Ask, "what do I want out of my life?"

This is an exercise that most people really suck at. You might say something like, "I want a Ferrari," or "I want a house with a pool," or "I want a body like (insert famous pop star's name OR Chris Hemsworth if you are a dude)."

You are doing it wrong.

Acquiring things might make you momentarily happy, but really, that's not where your lasting joy comes from. Material objects don't improve the experiences in your life. They don't make you better at your job. In the end, they are just things. And if given the choice between being able to go to Thailand (if guaranteed I would not get explosive diarrhea from merely drinking the water) or taking an object of equal value, I'm going for Thailand, baby (see diarrhea clause).

Why?

Because the value of your life is really about the relationships you have, how you grow as a person, and how you show up. It's not about what other people think about you: it's about if you are the type of person that others want to be around. Are you are filled with light and joy when you show up? Do you care about others and their struggles? Do you do the things you say you are going to do?

I know, we are not even two pages in and I am already asking you the tough questions. But this is stuff you really need to think about.

So, in order to be your best self, you need to get some things organized. It's as simple as that. You will undoubtedly end up wasting time if you aren't organized. You will lose sight of your goals without being organized. Being organized is pretty much the foundation for everything else, which is why it is the first chapter.

The problem is, some of us are very organized in some ways, but not in others. For example, you might know where every bill and paper in your house is, but your social life might be a mess. You might have scheduled several social outings with people you do not like and yes, unless you are immortal, this is a complete waste of your time. Ask yourself, "why do I allow this to happen?" If you don't enjoy their company or they don't inspire you to be better, then you probably shouldn't waste your time with them.

So let's talk about the areas of life where you need to be organized:

1. Your Schedule
2. Bills and Important Papers
3. Your Social Life
4. Your Material Possessions
5. Your Health
6. Your Work

SCHEDULE

Let's actually start with **your schedule**, because if that isn't right, nothing will be right. Essentially, you need to keep a schedule for pretty much every day of the week. I know that some of you are ready to now throw this book directly in the fire just based on this statement, but trust me and keep reading. Making a schedule might feel like just one more thing to do, BUT you are going to need it *even more* if you are always busy. It will help you to avoid feeling frenetic all of the time.

So let's review an example of how you might feel like your life is a mess, when it's really just got to do with how you schedule.. Imagine that you have to be at work at 9 am. It's very easy to NOT be at work on time, having absolutely nothing to do with how much time you left to get ready. If it takes you a half hour to commute to work, it's easy to wake up at 7:00, hit snooze until 7:30, start eating breakfast at 7:45, mindlessly watch cat videos until 8:20, and then be like, "holy shit! I have to leave in 10 minutes! How did this happen?" But if you look at people who *really get lots of things done in the same amount of hours that everyone else has in a day*, you will see a morning schedule that looks more like this if they have to be at work at 9am:
6 am wakeup and workout for 40 minutes
6:40 am write down goals for the day and visualize future success
7 am Breakfast
7:30 Spend time preparing to look polished for work
8:10 Leave the house and get to work early

See the difference? The second person is only getting up an hour earlier, but is accomplishing so much more.

If you want to make sure that you stick to this type of morning schedule, then set an alarm every time that you should be starting the next activity. For example, an alarm goes off at 6 to wake you and indicate that you should start your workout. Another alarm goes off at 6:40 so that you know to write down your goals and visualize your future success. Another alarm goes off to indicate that you should be eating breakfast and then another to indicate it's time to shower.

See how that works?

So let's look at how the days of our two sample people would be very different *based exclusively* on what they did in the morning.

The first person gets to work only 5-10 minutes late, but is frazzled. That person looks on her work calendar and realizes that she has a meeting she is about to be late for. That person also realizes that there is a lot that she should have done to prepare for the meeting to meet the goals in her work life. On top of it, the boss has left additional requests on the her desk for the day. This might potentially look as if she is having a really bad day. But all of this was COMPLETELY within her control. I will tell you what my business coach told me: a day is neither good nor bad. A day is agnostic. Sometimes we apply meaning because we don't want to take responsibility.

The organized person knew that the meeting was on the schedule, went through some talking points the night before, was in the office a few minutes early to settle and get her mind right, and so she crushes the meeting

Do you see what's going on here?

Let's continue with our example day.
The first person has to stay at work late because she didn't get everything done that she needed to get done. She wanted to go to the gym after work, but now it's too late and she doesn't feel like cooking, so she grabs some fast food. She heads home exhausted and watches tv for too long so that she falls asleep late and repeats the cycle again and again.

Meanwhile, the second person would be able to leave work on time and can use her evening to spend time with her children, meet up with friends, take a class that is meant to enrich her life or simply do some work around the house. Or if she is really ambitious, she now has the evening to work on a business she is running from home (something I recommend if you need to supplement your income). Maybe she is writing a book or wants to plan a trip. The possibilities are all there now that she has scheduled everything. And she only got up an HOUR earlier than the other person. Plus, she will be able to get to bed earlier since everything is done.

One major adjustment that will change your life: just stop watching tv on a regular basis. My husband and I have definitely noticed that we have more energy, better sleep and get more done when we abstain from television entirely. It's very easy to watch one episode of something and then it magically turns into three episodes (or even an entire season!) and everyone is then up too late and cranky the next day. Plus, an amazing thing happens when you turn the tv off: you actually talk to one another. OMG, I know. Weird, right? So you end up really developing your relationships in ways you may not have considered when you aren't losing a lot of time staring at a screen. We usually plan for a little tv or movie time on weekends, but think about it: aren't there better ways to spend your time?

Now I want you to bust out a pen and take a minute to write out an ideal (but doable) day. Do it now so that you don't keep any bad habits for even one more day.

Write out what you will do in every hour of the day. If you need to break it up so that you schedule every half hour instead, that is fine (maybe even better). Try to do this for a whole week. Scheduling things will also help you to avoid problems like "OMG that bill was due yesterday!" or communication problems like "I thought you were dropping our daughter off at sports tonight!" If everyone in the house has a schedule, it makes it so that roles and tasks become clearer. This can also take a lot of pressure off of your relationship. Notice that the schedule ends at 10 PM. That's because everyone should be at least PREPPING for bed at that time. I will be the first to admit that I am not often in bed by 10, but I also work 3-9:30 most days, so I try to begin winding things down by 10 as often as possible.

ACTION STEP: Plan a day

6am
7am

8am
9am
10am
11am
12pm
1pm
2pm
3pm
4pm
5pm
6pm
7pm
8pm
9pm
10pm

Now that you understand the importance of a schedule, let's talk about how we can get some other areas of your life together. Like your bills and papers.

BILLS AND IMPORTANT PAPERS

Organizing these things is a real problem for most people. This is how we end up not getting important things signed, missing deadlines, or overdrawing checking accounts. There are plenty of options for keeping organized on the computer, but some people do better with an old-fashioned filing cabinet. You have to know your personality and what will work better for you.

I do a combination. I have a filing cabinet for all the important statements and papers that come into the house via snail mail. Every single day, I file any papers that come in the mail in either the recycling bin or one of the hanging files in my filing cabinet. This takes all of about 5 minutes a day, and will save you hours and hours of searching. I hate having paper lying around. It not only looks cluttered, but it is pretty much a guarantee that something will get lost. Organizing these important items also prevents future drama and accusations. Fighting with your spouse or roommate over who put what where unfortunately doesn't make it magically appear. Filing it appropriately, however, does. True fact.

ACTION STEP: Your filing cabinet and hanging folders

Find a designated place for your filing cabinet and then label each of your hanging folders. You might use some of the following categories:

- Banking
- Investments
- Car
- Mortgage
- Homeowner's insurance
- Taxes
- Pay stubs
- Capital improvements on the house
- Continuing education
- Important school papers
- The deed to the house
- Will and testament
- Health Care Proxy
- Medical information/bloodwork etc.

You will certainly have more folders than that if you have your own business or if you have children. If you decide to get your children vaccinated for example, you need to keep records of that. If your children have any special needs and receive treatment or therapy through the school district, you will need to keep records of that as well. This looks more intimidating than it really is. On a scale of eating dinner with your in-laws to jumping out of a plane, it doesn't even register. It probably won't even take you a whole hour (less than the amount of time it would take you to eat dinner with your in-laws, but more time than it would take you to jump out of a plane).

If you are super tech savvy, you can definitely do this on the computer or possibly even on a tablet, but make sure that everything still has its own place and that you can find each folder easily. I actually often find it more difficult to find certain folders on the computer than I do in the filing cabinet. This might just be me, so do what you know will work best for you.

There is one thing that you don't want to put away in a filing cabinet however: bills. "Out of sight, out of mind" is probably good when it comes to erasing the memories of your ninety-year-old aunt stepping out of the shower, but it is very bad when it comes to paying your mortgage. Things that are not seen do not often get any attention. Don't believe me? When is the last time you wore those shoes in the back of your closet? I thought so. I have actually thrown shoes out that were in my husband's closet for too long and he STILL hasn't noticed (true). So let's make those bills (and their due dates) visible. You can also automate all of your reoccurring bills if that is easier for you. You can do this by having all of your bills automatically deducted from your checking account or charged to your credit cards. This is a great option if you don't trust your organizational skills or you know that you tend to forget to pay bills on time. Finally, you could set an alarm on your phone to remind you when each bill is due. Any of these are good options so pick one and use it religiously. Remember that paying bills on time affects your credit, so be proactive.

ACTION STEP: Get a piece of paper, some oaktag, a blackboard, or a dry erase board, and write the numbers 1-28 down the side vertically. Most bills will not be due on the 29th of the month because February doesn't have 29 days (most of the time). Next, look at the days of the month and next to every day, write the bills that are generally due that day. Once you know exactly what bills are due when, it makes it easier to budget and plan. Try to set aside a specific day and time to pay bills every week so that you never fall behind. On the day you pay your bills (let's say it's Friday), take care of all of the bills for the next seven days (if you are going on vacation, you need to plan for longer). Then when you sit down the following Friday, you will pay all of the other bills coming up until you sit down again the following week. If you don't use online banking, you need to leave yourself a little bit more time so that all of your payments get to the necessary places on time. Once you pay a bill, write the date that you paid it next to it every month. You can keep the same lists for several months (as long as due dates don't shift dramatically).

Example

1 Rent: 9/28, 10/27, 11/29
  Credit Card Bill: 9/28, 10/27, 11/29
2
3
4
5
6
7 Electric Bill 10/5, 11/4, 12/6
  Cable Bill   10/5, 11/4, 12/6

Repeat this for all of your reoccurring bills. Most of us also have bills that occur only occasionally, though. Examples would be medical bills, bills for work around the house, or random bills that come conveniently just as you have managed to save some money (the government seems to have radar for this sort of thing). So get ready for some sexy sexy organization here folks:

> For ancillary bills and all my paper bills, I have a shelf with one of these things:

Okay, so maybe it isn't SUPER sexy. What it is, though, is very practical (and sometimes practical IS sexy). I would recommend everyone get one or make one. It allows you to put all of your bills into a slot that represents the day they are due.

For my younger readers who don't really have very many bills yet, I would recommend employing a similar system for any school projects and papers that you have due. Adults can also use this type of system for any presentations or projects that might otherwise cause a complete stress fest at the last minute. So let's say you have a paper/presentation due on the 7th of the month. You would write out something like this:

Day 1 Read general ideas about topic of paper
     2 Write brief outline
     3 Detailed outline
     4 Rough draft
     5 Edit and revise
     6 Final edit
     7 Paper due

Got it? Nice. Let's move on to your social life.
SOCIAL LIFE

So this one is actually probably the hardest. We all have some wonderful people in our lives and we all have some vampires in our lives. When I talk about vampires here, they are definitely NOT the pretty *Twilight* kind, but rather, they are the people who suck your energy, have beliefs that no longer align with yours, fight with you constantly, encourage bad habits, bring you down, or are constantly asking favors while never doing anything in return. So really, they are more like parasites, I guess, since vampires would probably kill you.

Although, these people are kind of like killing you in a different way, I suppose.

I know, you are thinking about someone specifically right now.

Don't worry, that happens a lot.

It's also possible that you are thinking about a really toxic work environment where there are lots of people who are complaining, miserable parasites who never take any responsibility for anything they do (kind of like a room full of politicians).

If you are thinking about your spouse or your best friend, though, you are in trouble and we are going to talk about that in later chapters.

ACTION STEP: Start recognizing the positive influences in your life and the negative ones. I am a fan of writing things down, but if you'd like, you can just consider the following:

-Make a list of the people who are always supportive to you and love you regardless of your situation in life.

-Make a list of the people in your life whom you aspire to be like (you don't even have to necessarily know these people personally)

-Make a list of the people in your life who share your values and aspirations (these don't necessarily have to be people whom you are already friends with, these can be people whom you would like to be friends with)

-Make a list of the people in your life who lead a healthy lifestyle (and can help you do the same)

-Make a list of people who are always asking favors

-Make a list of people whom you dread seeing but see often anyway (you might be surprised at how many of these there are)

-Make a list of people who tend to bring you down whenever you see them.

-Here is a tough one: make a list of the people in your life who make excuses for you. This one is REALLY important, because it is often what stalls true progress in your goals. Do you eat a whole bag of chips and that person says something to the effect of "don't worry about it, you have had a rough day"? I have a few people in my life who do make excuses for me sometimes. They are often my biggest supporters and the people I love the most. In my case, I had to learn to block out their excuses and try to find out why I really didn't succeed. But maybe you have someone who is just constantly enabling your bad, lazy habits. This is something that you have to think seriously about and discuss. Excuses don't help anyone.

Finally, how are you scheduling your social life? In my particular case, I tend to find that I am either sitting in my house writing on a weekend, or my weekend is so socially packed that I can barely keep up. What I have gotten much better about, though, is refusing to hang out with people whom I don't enjoy seeing. That is a huge thing for me. I have also gotten really good about just leaving social events if I am really exhausted or have a lot to do the next day. You should give yourself the same courtesy. When I was out of state at a conference with my team, they had several nights where they went out late and went to a fancy dinner. Normally, this is the type of thing that I love, but I was sick as a dog with a terrible cold, dealing with a 3 hour time change, and was 3 months pregnant! So did I go to bed at like 8:00 every night? Yes, yes I did. Do I regret not going out with my team? No. I had to prioritize my own health an my baby's health. So I can hope that they don't think I am a snob, but either way, it wouldn't have made a difference. Care less about what other people think.

Speaking about what other people think, let's talk about how to avoid having tons of expensive crap that doesn't define you!

YOUR MATERIAL POSSESSIONS

Have you ever gotten really excited to get some shiny new object only to then realize that the satisfaction you obtain from purchasing said object is fleeting at best? Then you are cleaning stuff out of your house a year later, and you realize you would like nothing more than to be rid of said object?

Nope, that's not just you.

As a culture, we are kind of encouraged to buy lots of things. Our culture allows us to believe that buying things solves all sorts of problems, but, unless the things you are buying are books (which, let's face it, you can get most of those at the library), those things that you buy are eventually just going to fill up a landfill.

So here are two problems that most people have:
1. They own too much stuff
2. They don't have enough money

Do you see how two problems can be very easily resolved? If you buy less stuff, you will have more money. I know. Don't tell me: I am a genius.

Okay, no wait, that's just common sense.

But common sense, as they say, is not always common practice. Therefore, most people keep buying shit that they can't really afford and have no storage for. We will talk more about this in the chapters on money, but I am a strong proponent of making your money align with your value set. So, for example, my husband and I spend money on the following areas:

- Organic, high, quality foods
- Our dogs
- Life experiences
- Fitness
- Home remodeling or updating

- Skincare

We DO NOT spend money on the following
- Clothing (my mom has a thrift shop thing bordering on addiction, so there is no need to really ever purchase clothing)
- Furniture (see thrift shop thing)
- Purses (I don't need people looking at some brand name on my arm, seriously)
- Shoes (I had gotten all the shoes I will ever need by the age of 30, and now I am done: with the exception of sneakers for working out)
- Watches, jewelry or any other trinkets that are appealing initially but often just end up in a drawer

Studies have actually shown that it is just as satisfying to get rid of the stuff that you have accumulated as it is to go out and buy some new stuff. Imagine how amazing your house would look if you simply spent all of the time that you normally spend shopping getting rid of the unnecessary stuff that you already have. You can give it to the less fortunate or you can gift it to friends. You really don't need all of the stuff in your house/apartment. So here is what I suggest: if you haven't used it in several months, give it to someone who will use it. Similarly, if it no longer brings you joy, get rid of it. You definitely don't want it to feel like you materials are owning you. To me, there is nothing worse than feeling cluttered. My husband jokes that I would live in a house with a bed and one area to sit if it were up to me.

That's not really a joke, so much. I like my house to have as little in it as possible. My husband tends to be a little bit of a pack rat, though, so we have to do some compromising sometimes.

Why do I want to live like a monk? I do not attach myself to material possessions anymore (though I went through a phase of that: I think everyone does). You have to realize that your possessions ARE NOT who you are. They also DO NOT define you. I think a lot of people will look at someone who owns a Rolex watch and think, "wow, that's someone who is wealthy and has their shit together." I will look at that same person and think, "wow, that is someone who is trying to define himself by what he owns, and probably has his priorities a little out of order." Or, after having read a lot about how people tend to spend their money, I would probably think "that is someone who probably has massive credit card debt."

That may seem harsh, but think about it. If you can afford a Rolex, which is something like $50,000, I want you to think about all of the good that you could do in the world for that same amount of money. I am not even talking about necessarily donating that money, but I am saying that, instead of working 20-hour days to pay for that, you could work less and maybe spend more time with your loved ones. Or maybe you can go on the vacation of a lifetime. Or maybe you now have so much money that you can start spending some time volunteering or pursuing your hobbies. Do you see where I am going? In the end, a Rolex is just a thing. If you gave me one tomorrow, I would probably try to sell it so I could have the money to adopt a child. If a sound like a hippy here, that's fine. But let me tell you, THINGS don't EVER make people happy in the long run. Good relationships, a purposeful life, and good experiences make people happy. There's research on it.

You're welcome.

The other thing that will really cut down on the material possessions that won't serve you is to ask friends and family to respectfully not buy you anything during the holidays. We usually swap out an experience. For example, we will all go to a hockey game together. Or we will all go to a Broadway play and dinner together. Or one year my husband surprised me with a trip to Aruba for Christmas (you can bet that was better than any ring or trinket he could have gotten me).

Here is the other problem with owning lots of stuff: not only do you have to pay for it, but now you have to ORGANIZE it. Yes, that is why your garage and your basement start to look like they belong to a hoarder and you can't find your children under the piles of crap lying all over the place. You want stuff? Better figure out where to put it!! And you better do it in such a way that you won't be wondering what the hell you did with it if you actually do need it.

So my best organization advice to you when it comes to material possessions?

Throw. Shit. Out.

Just saying. You probably will only use that stuff once anyway.

So here's the thing: define what you value most in life. For us, it's health, family, and happiness. If you are about to buy something that does not align with those values, stop yourself. You don't need it. You won't miss it. Trust me on this. You are not that cool for having a Lou Voitton bag or whatever those high heels are that women are nuts over that cost like a grand. Ask yourself, more importantly: why do you want it? If you want it for a shallow reason, then let it go and work on WHY you have that shallowness in you. Or perhaps, WHY it is that you want to APPEAR better than other people or appear that you can afford more than other people. Why is that so important?

Truth bomb: it's not.

When you become absorbed in what really matters, you will find that your possessions mean nothing. You can look nice for $40 or you can look nice for $1000, and most observers won't even know the difference. A ten-year-old car can get you safely from place to place or a brand new Mercedes can get you from place to place. Why do you need the Mercedes? You don't. You have been told you do by clever advertising. Don't buy into it.

So what do you really need?

Your health, your family, coping mechanisms for when times get tough, and a network of people who support your dreams.

But let's focus on health next

HEALTH

I am about to drop a huge secret on you right here, right now. It is the secret to longevity, looking younger, having better energy, losing weight, and getting more out of your life in general:

You have to eat right and exercise.

I know. You are shocked. You are so surprised that you actually started going into seizures. It's appalling. You have never heard such a thing.

It is true.

I think the thing that confuses most people is HOW to eat well and exercise. Most people start with a gym membership, and that is a HUGE mistake. If you get a gym membership, that means that you will also need to find time to GET to the gym. Once at the gym, you will have to actually know what you are doing. Then you will have to leave extra time to get home from the gym. Based on all of this, you know that you will come up with forty excuses for not going to the gym. Do you know what would be so much more convenient and realistic? If you just worked out in your house with limited equipment: first thing when you wake up in the morning.

This makes it really hard to miss a workout and it makes excuses really hard to come by, even if your schedule is jam packed. Anyone can buy some resistance tubing, do a half hour of P90X3 5 days a week, and start looking all ripped up. It's not very complicated. All you have to do is get Beachbody Streaming On Demand, and that will allow you to have access to over 600 workouts geared towards all different skill levels. Here is a link:
https://www.teambeachbody.com/shop/d/BODStandalone?referringRepID=1398383

So instead of going to a gym, waiting 20 minutes for a treadmill that someone else just sweat all over and getting a sub-par workout, you can have a different trainer-guided workout that is made for your particular skill level IN YOUR HOUSE. I mean, seriously. I used to train people in their homes, and they paid big bucks for that. The cost of Beachbody on Demand FOR THE YEAR is less than what it would cost PER SESSION with a personal trainer. Are you thinking "no-brainer" here? Yes, that's because you can read and you are smart. Better get on that, now.

So that's half of the equation taken care of. Easy peasy. Now we have to address the eating and nutrition part. I know. It's like walking into a cave with no light sometimes. It can get kind of complicated.

So why? Why is the eating thing so complicated?

Simply put, it is because there is just so much bad information out there, and there are also a million people who are trying to sell you things. Some people will tell you to eliminate carbs completely, or eliminate sugars completely, or eliminate fats completely. I love the programs that tell you to go get a little scale and start weighing all of your food: because that's realistic. That's definitely something you have time for. Better yet, do that for your whole family! They will *be totally* supportive. No wait, what's the opposite of that? They will hate you. That's it. They will hate you.

Oh but I am not done enumerating the many different forms of insanity that pass as nutritional plans. Have you thought about getting pre-packaged frozen meals with enough preservatives in them to practically embalm you? Because who needs the Dead Sea with that much sodium? Also, you don't really need to engage yourself in the social component of eating. Not you. It's just you and the good ol' microwave. Nothing says "potential crazy cat lady (or dude)" like a microwaved meal for one.

I mean, seriously?

Think really hard for a minute. Do you know anyone who has sustained ANY of these lifestyles? This is completely different from someone who has lost a little weight and then gained it back. Losing weight and then gaining it back is easy to do. Anyone can do that.

Do you know anyone who has gone like 10 years with no carbs? Didn't think so. Do you know anyone who has gone totally low fat for long periods of time and then actually gained weight?

Yup. This is more realistic.

I think that most of you know that I am vegan and it is the best decision I have ever made for my health. But I do realize that being vegan is not for everyone. Even though it is the best thing for your heart, your health, and the planet, some people struggle with it.

If you are eating animals, try to go mostly plant-based at least. This is much better for your heart and your overall health. But even as a vegan, it is possible to overeat. It is possible to overeat with any meal plan, despite what other people may tell you (lies). Whenever you hear "you can eat as much bacon as you want!" run screaming. Eating as much bacon as you want is a sure way to get your cholesterol to skyrocket. Also, remember the old adage "you are what you eat?" Yeah, put two and two together there.

Thankfully, there is a system of eating that works well with anyone's lifestyle. It is the Beachbody Portion Fix Container system. You can use the containers at home, or when you go out. By doing ONE DAY of simple calculations and reading through a little tiny book, you will know exactly how many portion containers to use every day.

It is like magic. Seriously, it is as close as you will ever get to being able to wave a magic wand and have the weight magically fall off. Want the link for the portion containers?

https://www.teambeachbody.com/shop/d/beachbody-portion-control-7-piece-container-kit-BBPortionControlContainer?referringRepID=1398383

But here's the thing. If you are sticking to a nutritional program, but still not getting all of the micronutrients that you need (for those of you who have read *Unleash Your True Athletic Potential*, you know how I am obsessed with nutrient density and micronutrients), you will still feel hungry at times and have cravings for all sorts of garbage. Thankfully, Beachbody has thought of everything and made a vegan version of something called Shakeology. This is a shake that you can use as a meal replacement or a supplement. I use it for dinner most nights because I am usually working during dinner time. It also tastes like dessert to me, so it fills in any gaps that might be in my nutrition while satisfying cravings. Did I mention that it is really easy to make a shake and take it anywhere? Well it totally is. Done! What's that? You need a link?

https://www.teambeachbody.com/shop/d/vegan-shakeology-barista-combo-SHKComboCHVVNVCLVegan?referringRepID=1398383

All kidding aside, I was lucky enough to be introduced to Beachbody, and it has really changed the way I organize my workouts, my nutrition, and my life. Here is why it is awesome and will organize the fitness and health component of your life for you. With Beachbody you have the option of getting:

- Coach support
- Portion Containers for at home OR eating out
- Access to over 600 workouts
- Shakes for when you don't have time and need nutrition

I think the only way it would actually be simpler is if someone came to your house and moved your legs for you while you were working out. Or cooked all of your meals for you. I mean, good luck with that. Take what you can get.

But you know, sometimes things like work can get in the way of your nutrition and your workouts, so let's organize that next.

WORK LIFE

Okay, so I have some kind of weird advice for you. Have a business (even if it is a very small one) that you have in your home. The tax deductions for this (talk to an accountant who specializes in this area) can be amazing. But having a home-based business (even part of the time) allows you to follow your passion. If you want to know about my home-based business and how I love it and am successful with it, please email me at juliannesoviero@gmail.com. The thing of it is, that having something that allows you to follow your passion and make money can provide a very welcome relief from your day to day work. I happen to love being an athletic performance consultant, but my home-based business lets me work on something else that I love.

Maybe you are passionate about makeup and skincare. You don't need a lot of money or to buy a lot of products for your home-based business. You simply need to have passion for it and find a team of people who are also passionate about it. Maybe you are passionate about nutrition and fitness (email me!). Maybe you are passionate about fixing things or refinishing furniture and can give great advice about it. Can you monetize it? Yes, yes you can.

I recognize that you might not want to heed some of that advice either because you already have your own business or you just love working for the man. There are some things that you can do to organize your work life that will really make a big difference for you, whether you have your own business or you are working for someone else.

1. **Stay away from Negative Nancies**: Yes, this includes the people who talk smack about everyone else, AND the people who can't stop complaining about how they hate working for the company you work for or how your boss is an asshole or how their life is a mess. Being around these types of people constantly will dampen your spirits and will make you think that those negative things about other people are legit (even if they aren't true at all).
2. **Schedule breaks at work**: Let's just be clear that this isn't some kind of procrastination party. It's more like rewarding yourself for a job well done. So for example, if you have been on your grind for like 2 hours at a computer screen, it would really help you to stand up and do a little stretching. This is also something that will really help you to improve

your health and fitness. Don't take this time to kibbitz with every living human around the water cooler, because that is how those Negative Nancies stalk their prey. Taking a little break at work is NOT an excuse to just zone out with cat videos or talk to your neighbor about some television series. It is YOUR time to refresh and allow your creativity to get going. Either plan on a little physical movement or meditation. My guidance counselor in junior high school used to take her lunch break to go running every day. I thought that was just so cool. In retrospect, thinking about the benefits to her health and her mental clarity, I think it is even cooler.

3. **Plan out every day:** Not every day will be perfect, unfortunately. Clients will cancel, people will call out last minute, or you might be called upon to do EXTRA during your day. That's okay. If you take a few moments to plan ahead of time, get to work early, and map out your day, you will be more productive, and more relaxed. Trust me here. Getting up a little earlier will make you feel like superman with regards to how much you are getting done at work.

4. **Develop good rapport with your team or coworkers:** Okay, this is where it is time for me to be honest. As a college athlete, whenever we were assigned group projects, I always used the excuse of my practice and game schedule to get out of group projects:

    Me: "I know that we are supposed to work with partners (or in groups or whatever) on this project, but my practice schedule would make it nearly impossible for me to meet with others. I'm not trying to do less work than the rest of the class, I can do the whole project by myself, but I was hoping that I could do it on my own."

    Professor: "Are you sure? That's a lot of work."

    Me: "Yes. I am aware. I wouldn't want to impose on my group by not being able to make meetings."

In case you are wondering: yes, this worked every time. I literally got out of every single group project ever assigned to me in college. My logic was that, in the past, I had always done ALL of the work for the group projects anyway, so I might as well get credit for all of it. I also hated trying to organize other people, and yes, my practice schedule was pretty prohibitive. Did I mention that I am a Type A personality?

Here's the thing: in college, there are slackers. There might be some of those on your team at work too. That sucks and, yes, you will end up doing most of the work. However, when you find some people whom you can TRULY work with as a team, your life will change. And when I say "find" people that you can truly work with, I really mean "make" them.

Let me explain. I have had my own full-time business now for nearly 15 years. For the first several years, I was entirely by myself. I would catch for the girls, teach, and schedule. I loved it, but it could be frustrating because I had the sense that I could do more AND I was scheduling 6 days a week, because I had to do EVERYTHING. Fast forward to when I heard about another pitching instructor using some of her older athletes to warm up her pitchers and THEN she would work with them. I didn't know. Could I organize things that way? Could I give up that much control? It seemed daunting, but, even though my athletes had been outrageously successful, I felt like there was something missing in my business.

It was teamwork.

So I took some of the athletes whom I thought were the best suited to teaching and groomed them. Then I made them independent contractors. They began warming my athletes up and sharing their own unique perspective. You can probably guess what happened: I was happier, my athletes performed EVEN BETTER, and having more input in several different areas was exactly what I needed. I don't think I could ever going back to doing it the way I used to. Sure, there was some trial and error at first. I definitely found that I could make most athletes with a pitching background great teachers if they concentrated and were present with their pitchers. On the other hand, I couldn't fix potential instructors who were on their phone 24/7 and not paying attention to the young athletes who really needed their help. So I kept working with the girls who were really passionate about what they did, and I let the others find their own way. That brings me to my next point.

Be passionate about what you do!
 Look, everyone has something they can be passionate about that others would consider "work." I once had another pitching instructor ask me if I was "bored" teaching the same thing day in and day out to pitchers. I told him that I was never bored because every girl is unique and should be taught differently. Also, because athletes have different body types, and different needs, I found that was I constantly being challenged with trying to be creative. This told me something about HIM as a pitching instructor, though: that he DID teach most people the same way. So basically, what I am saying is: don't be that guy. Literally. Be passionate about what you do. If you aren't passionate, start looking at things that you are passionate about and brainstorm ways that it might generate income. You never know where that may lead.

Now that you are totally organized, let's get on to those goals!!!!!!

2 GOOALLLLSSS!!!!!

Setting goals is one of those things that everyone will tell you to do. I am definitely not the first person to tell you to set goals. You will also hear that you have to make your goals
-specific
-measureable
-attainable

So I am not going to repeat all of that. What I will do is place emphasis on the fact that most of us do NOT keep our goals in sight (or in our minds) on a regular basis, and that is why we are stuck in the same patterns again and again. We also often make goals only in our own minds, and don't share these goals with people, which takes away from our accountability.

The thing about goals that is crazy is that I don't even think that they have to necessarily be "attainable." Why? Because people thought a 4 minute mile was impossible. Flight was also thought to be impossible for a long time. Even if other people think it is impossible (and trust me, everyone wants to tell you about how your dreams are impossible). The thing is that if YOU believe you can do it, and you have persistence that just doesn't ever quit, you will reach your goals eventually.

When I first wanted to open up my business, I could remember someone saying, "if that were a really good idea, then someone else would have already done it."

Imagine if someone had said that to the people who were harnessing electricity!

The point is, I have had a successful business for well over a decade now, despite the fact that haters gonna hate.

Think about what you should REALLY be asking yourself before you set a goal:
1. **Do I REALLY want this** (if you don't, you will go after it half-assed, and we want you to go after your goals full-assed)?
2. **Am I willing to spend as much time as is necessary to achieve this goal?** Timelines for certain goals are reasonable. If an athlete comes to me and wants to gain 5 mph, after I have known that athlete for only a few weeks, I can give her a timeline for that goal. But if your goal is to pay off your mortgage and buy a house in Kaui, then you are talking about a goal that will take you several years (as opposed to several weeks or months), so be prepared for that. Similarly, if you want to lose 50 pounds, that will safely occur in about 25 weeks, so you have to be willing to be vigilant for that entire time. I was willing to go full-throttle on my goal of creating online income for about two and a half years, but after hours and hours (and essentially only breaking even), I decided that particular goal was no longer important to me. See how this works? Set a timeline. You will be glad you did.
3. **Is this goal something that will really enhance my life?** So many people make goals that are very perfunctory. Would losing weight enhance your life, or are you doing it because others want you to do it? If you don't believe in the ability of the goal to enhance your life, then it is pointless to invest your energy into it.
4. **Are you willing to put your resources into seeking help for your goal?** Learning better investing strategies and money management often requires you to either read about it a bunch or hire someone. The same goes for weight loss or any other skill you want to perfect. I want to be able to speak Spanish fluently in two year's time. I have been learning bits and pieces of Spanish for years, but once I set a timeline and said "I'm going to be fluent in two years!" then I really started allocating my resources to my goal and therefore work on it every single day.

Most people unfortunately do NOT achieve their goals, and there are reasons why:
1. **The goal doesn't have enough meaning**. When you set a goal, ask yourself *why* you are setting the goal. Does Aunt Wilma really want you to do it? Do you feel external pressure? If the goal doesn't have some deep emotional resonance for you or doesn't come from you personally then you are probably going to fail at it. For example, if you want to lose weight so that you can look a little bit better, that's really different than if you want to lose weight because you are invited to your ex's wedding in two months and you want to stun in whatever you are wearing. I mean, let's be honest. If you don't have a really strong reason for doing what you do, it probably won't get done at all.
2. **You don't have any accountability.** You need people whom you are going to tell about your goals. Those people should support you, but should also get on your ass if you don't do what you say you are going to do. These shouldn't be the "it's okay, you have a million excuses" type of people. These need to be the people who are looking at you when you make excuses and saying, "that's not how you said you were going to live your life from now on." That might be hard to hear, but it is often what we need to make us achieve our full potential.
3. **You haven't set up the right "sprints."** If you have a goal that is going to take two years, it is easy to keep putting things off because you figure you have two years to achieve the goal. Break it down into daily tasks or two week intervals filled with tasks that will lead to achievement of your overall goal. So a good plan for achieving a goal would go something like this:
    - Set ONE big goal. Let's just say that it is paying off your student loans.
    - Establish a reasonable timeline. How long will this really take to achieve? For this example, let's say that paying off your student loans would take you two years. Now because that goal is VERY long term, it would be easy to lose sight of it, and keep

deferring and doing all sorts of nasty things that would continue to put you further into debt. Instead, make 2 week "sprints" for your goals. I got this idea courtesy of Whitney Hansen (whom I really like, look her up). The first "sprint" might consist of two weeks where you focus on creating and marketing an online course to help you make a little more money (all of which would go towards paying off the loans). Each day for those two weeks, you would have an actionable task to keep you on the right track. The next two weeks, you might read a book about how to make the most of your finances, or you might start doing some research on EFTs and how they can help you to achieve your goal of getting out of debt. I think that you get the idea. You need a goal, but then you need a map of things to do every day.

4. **You are focusing on too many goals at one time**. I am very guilty of this particular practice. I want to do so much that I make forty goals, and then only make minimal progress on all of them instead of making huge progress on one. By just focusing on one goal over the last few weeks, I can't believe how much progress I have been making. more than I had made over the last year in that one area!!

5. **The people whom you spend the most time with are sabotaging you**. This is sad, but often very common. We are generally most like the people whom we spend the most time with, but we also let them affect us the most. I used to train an incredibly successful author who wanted to lose weight. He used to make really good progress with losing weight until he would go to hang out with his friends. They were mostly overweight and would make comments about how good he looked after losing weight, while simultaneously encouraging him to have a slice of 1,000 calorie cheesecake. I mean, really. You can't make this up. This is why the best predictor of whether or not you are overweight has absolutely nothing to do with genetics or even what diet you are on. The best predictor by far is how heavy your friends are. True fact. So get your friends a copy of this book so that they stop

eating like crap and not exercising. They are dragging you down with them.
6. **You are simply not ready to accept the achievement of your goal**. This one is HUGE! So many of us are actually a little scared to achieve our big goals. I mean, if we achieve our biggest goals, what will be left for us to do? Or, worse, we have these limiting beliefs that have been ingrained into us from birth about how everything good that we achieve SHOULD be difficult.. Or we self-sabotage. If any of this sounds like you, here are some things you might want to look into that can help you:
    - Hypnosis
    - NLP
    - Havening
    - Therapy
    - A life coach
    - Meditation

So this is a section of the book that you should keep referring to again and again because you are going to need it every time that you make a new goal. Right now, I want you to JUST focus on the MOST IMPORTANT goal that you would like to achieve. Once you have accomplished that, you can use this method for each subsequent goal you make.

Fill out the following:

Goal:

Why is it important?:

No really. WHY is it important? (keep asking yourself, because if it isn't important enough, it will never get done).

How long will it take to achieve this goal? If you don't know how long it will take, talk with others who have achieved similar goals. They will **WANT** to help you. Ask them how long it took. Ask them how they did it.

Break your goal down into "sprints." Right now, you can set up the first two week sprint, and then, as you see what works and what doesn't, begin setting up your next set of sprints:

Decide who your support system is. If you don't have one, you need to **GET ONE**. It is so important to have people who will encourage you and support you on the road to success. Don't pick people who will be jealous of your success down the road (see #5 above for more information)

Bust out a calendar. It can be on your phone or it can be made with real, live paper. Every day, put a reminder of exactly what you want to achieve. Set an alarm on your phone every day to remind you of your mission and to keep you working towards this goal. Right now, (that's right, right this second: put the book down) write down something on every day of your calendar (even if it's just a small task) to help you move towards your goal. Do this for the next two weeks.

Don't worry, I will wait. Go for it

3 WHERE ALL YOUR DAMN MONEY IS GOING

Okay, be honest. How many of you just looked at the title of this chapter and wanted to skip it completely? Yup. We either hate talking about money or we love it. I definitely do find that it is more socially acceptable to lament about how broke you are than it is to brag about how you're rolling in the cheddar. There is a lot of stigma around money sometimes. I felt like I personally didn't' have great thoughts about people with lots of money because, when I was about twelve, we moved from a neighborhood where everyone seemed to earn about the same (and we were close with our neighbors) to a neighborhood where we didn't even know our neighbors and there was definitely some snobby, elitist nonsense going down.

So you know, I work through my own stuff, sometimes, too. I am not perfect.

Yet.

This seismic shift in location as a young adult really shaped my thoughts about money, and I recently realized that I often associated being wealthy with being elitist, selfish, racist, and oftentimes, lonely. I didn't have any friends at all in our new location, but prior to moving, I had lots of friends literally right down the block. So let's be honest: most of us have hang ups about money in some way or another. Finding the root of those hang ups can literally change your life. My hang ups about money partially have to do with how I took those silly little microcosmic things that happened in my youth and extrapolated them to the entire world at large. Imagine taking the loneliest, most miserable part of your life and basing your financial perspectives on everything that happened during that time. Maybe you ARE doing that right now and it's holding you back!!! Think about it: seriously. I thought that most rich people were complete d-bags. Did I want to be like that? NO! So I created some self-sabotaging behavior surrounding money. I so badly wanted to not look like a complete tool that I would often act apologetic for making money. If I was talking about a vacation that I was going on and people said something like "good for you!" I would usually qualify my awesome vacation by saying something like, "well we got a really great deal" or "it's only for a few days."

That's a really silly way to go through life, if you think about it.

So before we dig really deep into some action steps that you can take to set yourself up for long term financial success, ask yourself the following questions:

1. What are my hang-ups about money and where did they come from?
2. What are my most important financial goals and (even more importantly), WHY am I interested in achieving them? If you are wanting lots of money so that you can be strolling around in Prada or showing off your Mercedes, you probably aren't going to be as successful as someone who wants to get lots of money so that she can quit a job that makes Hades look like a resort in Bora Bora. Just saying.
3. What is your language around money like? Remember how I mentioned NLP (Neuro linguistic programming) earlier in the book? The idea behind NLP is that our words literally shape our reality. So if you keep saying things like "I'm broke" or "I'm terrible with money," that will shape your reality. Start saying things like, "Ima beast this credit card debt!" or "I am learning how to be a rock star with money!" As you do that, watch your reality start to change. Also be mindful of how the people around you talk about money, since they will often mirror your language and your behavior (and vice versa). I have been really conscientious over the past several months about this and have therefore purposefully made connections with people who have healthy approaches to money and

finances. This meant reaching out to other entrepreneurs and even joining a group of women who have done amazing things in their professional lives. This has done wonders for my thinking about money and business. If you feel that there is no way that you can have any positive language about money, we are going to explore that in a minute. We will talk about why sometimes it feels like there are holes in your wallet or how, no matter how much you make, you feel like you are just treading water, but, for now, just try to notice how your language and the language of those around you is shaping your financial reality.

4. The people whom you spend the most time with: what are their values like when it comes to money? Are you friends with people who will go out to a bar, buy three fancy drinks that looks like someone made them with a glow sticks or unicorn tears, and then talk about how they have trouble making the mortgage that month? I definitely know people who have luxury cars that complain about their everyday bills. Or people who spend hundreds of dollars on clothes and then wonder why they have no savings. Or people who go on vacations that they can't afford. Don't feel bad or start flogging yourself if you fall into one of these categories, because you might not even realize that you have been doing something like this (since so much of our behavior is subconscious), but if your friends do this sort of stuff, you probably will too. On the other hand, if your friends are responsible and successful with diversified stocks, mutual funds, a healthy savings account, and a clear vision for their financial future, they will force you to level up.

So what are some active steps you can take to help you to be a boss with money? First of all, you should totally geek out about it: read about it, love it, and respect it. When I first got married, I knew NOTHING about money. I learned everything I know by reading, reading and reading. Second, I am going to share with you some of the simple steps that I have done so that money isn't really a huge concern anymore. It's not that I don't EVER stress about money, but I did all of the steps below in my mid-twenties, so now, only a few years later (okay, more like 13 years later), I have resources that are literally building themselves automatically. Everything is deducted from my accounts without me having to take any additional action, and because of compounding interest, it just keeps growing.

Now I want to help *you* as much as I can. One of the things that I have realized over the years is that it's nice to feel like you are making a lot of money, but you don't *need* to make a lot of money to *have* a lot of money. You just have to be smart and exercise a little discretion. I have also realized that much of the advice in financial books is very redundant and the basics can therefore be covered in one chapter. You can learn more about any area that applies to you by taking a few notes as you read today and then researching the areas that you think you need help in. Here are the basics about managing finances, and how they can work for you:

1. **Evaluate your spending habits**: This has got to be the most important thing you can do for yourself. It will answer that question that you are always asking: "where the hell is all my money going?" There is usually at least one category where you spend a lot of money and you don't even realize it. The craziest thing about this sort of spending is that it very often doesn't even improve your quality of life. Most of the time, you just do it out of habit. For example, let's say you eat out for lunch and dinner every day. So maybe that's about $30 a day, but that can be around $900 a month (yikes!). So how do you discover your big, dirty secret? You MUST write down absolutely everything that you spend in a little notebook (or, if you wanna get fancy, put it in your phone). Carry this little notebook with you at all times, and ANYTIME you purchase ANYTHING (even a pack of gum), write it down. Then, at the end of every week, look at what you spent your money on, and next to each purchase put either a plus sign, a minus sign, or a circle. The plus sign means it was a good use of your money. The minus sign means that it was not a good use of your money OR you could get it cheaper elsewhere. The circle means that you aren't sure or that you are indifferent about it. Simply the act of having to track absolutely everything you spend will often deter you from spending on the things that you don't really

want or need. At the end of every week, you will also total all of your purchases and expenses for the week. You will use this to cut out things that you really don't need and also to inform your future buying decisions. To get a good idea of where all of your money is going right now, print out your credit card statements and bank statements. Give all of your purchases the same rating system described above. If you want to take things a step further, though, use some fun colored highlighters to help categorize all of your expenses. Highlight all food expenses in blue, all entertainment expenses in yellow, all utility bills in orange, all clothing bills in pink, all pet expenses in chartreuse, and so on. You get the idea. When you are done with this fun coloring exercise, you will know EXACTLY where all of your money is going and you can make decisions about how to cut down your expenditures on the things that don't correspond with your life values. For example, if you really want to travel, but you find that you spend $300 a month on clothing, your life values and your spending habits are out of line. Don't beat yourself up over it, just begin to make your adjustments. When I first started doing these exercises, I was shocked at how much I was spending on gym memberships (yes, plural) and things at Sephora. Though fitness is so important to me, I looked at those numbers and then decided to do all of my workouts at home instead of going to two different gyms. This saved me something like $2000 a year!!!!! With the Sephora habit, I decided stick to only two brands that I really like and only buy them when they are on sale or when I completely run out. That also saved me several hundred dollars a year. Do either of these changes detract from my life in any way? No: quite the opposite. When I see the money that I would have spent on silly things generating compound interest every month, it is really exciting and empowering. Trust me: you too will easily find a few things in your spending habits that you will be able to eliminate. Amazingly enough, you will have more money in your bank account (or index funds or retirement accounts) AND you will find that the money that you had once spent on silly expenses can now be used to build your future.

2. **Know exactly how much it costs you to live**: If you had NO other expenses at all every month, how much does it cost you to have shelter, food, and transportation? When you know this number, it makes it much easier to plan. You will find that you aren't short when it comes to paying the mortgage/rent and you will never be at risk for having the electricity turned off on you. Fact: if you know exactly what bills are coming and when, you are going to be able to plan for that every single month. No more acting indignant when the oil bill comes and then scrambling to figure out how you will pay it. "Who used all of this electricity?" you might have wondered with surprise every time. Um, *you* did, actually. And you would know your patterns of use if you simply took some time to look through your monthly expenses.
3. **Pay in cash**: This also makes a huge difference in your spending habits. If you put $200 on your credit card, you probably won't really think very much about it until you get the bill. Even then, you might put off paying it (or just pay the minimum). Incidentally, this is one of the fastest ways to get into massive credit card debt and ruin your life. If you shell out 10 Andrew Jacksons, you can bet you are going to be thinking about it just a bit more. I would also strongly recommend that you NEVER EVER carry a credit card balance from month to month. Seriously. This can be kind of hard at first, but, if you pay for more things in cash, your credit card bills will not be as high to begin with. Then simply use the following rule: don't put more on your credit card every month then you can pay off the following month. I also have only three credit cards: one for my business, one for personal use, and one for cash advances. That's it. If you have 20 credit cards, it might be time to make some phone calls and bust out the scissors. That's right: cut those bad boys up and embrace your newly found freedom. Just be mindful if you are about to go looking for a home loan: closing some credit cards might affect your credit rating (so does opening up new cards). Most financial experts suggest that you check your credit rating at least once a year, so that you can make some adjustments if it is not where it should be. Knowing you're credit score can help you to curb your

spending, but it is good to know for other reasons as well. For example, the interest rates on your credit cards might actually be higher than those of someone with a very good credit rating. That can be something that really affects your ability to pay your card (or cards) off. Speaking of debt...

4. **Get Rid of Debt, Pronto:** Okay, this is a tough one. The average American household has over $130,000 in debt. For most households, that includes about $15,000 in credit card debt and most cardholders rack up about another $1,000 in debt around the holiday season. Holy Shit!!! I mean that's $1,000 worth of stuff that will probably end up in a basement or landfill at some point in your lifetime anyway. What are we thinking? If you are following the rule of only putting what you can afford on your credit card every month, then the credit card debt will not be an issue for you. If you already have substantial credit card debt, make it your mission to pay off the card with the highest rate first. Another thing you can do is get an introductory offer for a new credit card that has zero percent interest for a year or more, use that to transfer your balance of the card with the highest interest, and then pay off that balance before the introductory offer expires. You just have to be aware that doing these sorts of things affects your credit ratings, so if you are about to buy a house or go for a car loan, talk to a financial advisor before doing this. Me, I have been busting ass to pay off my hubby's student loans, and I will sometimes wait for one of y credit cards to make me an offer of zero percent interest on cash advances for 12 months, and then I will ask for a large sum of money and use it to pay down the loan. Considering that the loan is at nearly eight percent interest, this saves me A LOT of money in the long term. But debt is a very serious issue when it comes to your overall financial health. Debt can be in credit cards, student loans, car payments, and (yes) even your mortgage is debt. Being unable to pay your debts can become a huge and ongoing problem, so tackle that sucker right away. For more on this topic, I would recommend David Bach's book, *Debt Free for Life*.

5. **Pay Yourself First:** According to Market Watch, about 62% of Americans have less than $1,000 in their savings accounts,

and 21% don't even have a savings account. OMG, where is that emoji that's rolling it's eyes? Saving is not that difficult. Even if you only make $150 a week, you must make it a priority to PAY YOURSELF FIRST. So what does this mean? Make it so that a portion of what you make automatically goes into savings, a portion automatically goes into mutual funds, and a portion automatically goes into retirement. With compounding interest, a little goes a long way over time.

6. **Make Your Money Generate Income**: I did my homework over ten years ago to find an Oppenheimer Fund that I still invest into every month. The dividends keep reinvesting and will eventually create a monthly income for me. Isn't that neat? You can do it too! At the time of my research, I chose something that suited my personality: that meant something that wasn't very high risk or a huge initial investment. So I started with just $500. Now that I have done more financial research, I will probably soon switch those funds out for more aggressive funds given that I don't expect to be taking income from them any time soon. To find out what funds might be right for you, definitely do your homework! You might want to sit down and speak with a financial advisor: just be aware that many financial advisors are paid commissions to refer you to certain products. Those products/funds are best for them, but what would be best for YOU? You might be very young and want to invest in something high-risk so that you have the potential for greater returns. You might be older and want something really conservative. Regardless, you want something where money is automatically taken from your checking account every month, the profits are reinvested, and you can start using the account to create monthly income in several years. I mean, hello: your money is making money. What's better than that?

7. **Have multiple sources of income/revenue**: You might have a really secure job with a pension, but it still shouldn't be your only source of income. This is important because there will be times in your life when cash flow in one area will slow down or even stop altogether. For example, you might lose your job or the stock market might tank. If you had lots

invested in either area, you might feel like you want to scream and cry and writhe on the floor while drooling and shaking. I mean, I hear you, but if you have multiple sources of revenue, then you don't really have to panic. There are lots of ways that you can have a little extra money coming in: even if it's only an extra $30 a week. Here are some ideas:

- Take a hobby and begin to monetize it. Do you like fixing up old furniture? Then begin charging a little for it.
- Join an MLM (make sure that it is a product that you are really passionate about and that the company has a good reputation).
- Create some online courses. Do you know how to do something that lots of other people don't know how to do? Maybe you are great with wiring or tile or fixing cars. Monetize that knowledge! It costs very little to create online courses and they can be a great source of income.
- Sell your unwanted stuff on Ebay or Craigslist.
- Become involved in real estate investing (make sure that you do lots of homework and asses the risk/rewards if this is something that you are interested in)

Try whatever you feel most comfortable doing. It takes several years to get to a point where you have multiple streams that really make a dent in your bills, but it's worth it. If still aren't sure what might be good in terms of creating extra income for you, here are my multiple streams (not including stocks and mutual funds):
      a. Private lessons/consultations
      b. Havening/hypnosis
      c. Royalties from my books
      d. Online programs
      e. Beachbody

So yes, most of this might not make me a millionaire tomorrow, but every little bit counts, and when I think my business account is at nearly zero and then a Beachbody payment or an Amazon payment comes in, it is definitely cause for celebration and gratitude.

8. **Life insurance**: Alright, so this is really more about protecting your partner or your loved ones in case something

happens to you, but there are certain life insurance policies that you can pay into and then cash in if you don't use them by a certain age. I have a compilation of life insurance policies. I have one that I paid into for about ten years and now covers me for most of my life (and I don't have to pay it anymore). I have another that is automatically deducted from my checking account and generates interest (though not a huge amount), and I could decide to "cash out" of it if I would like. These are whole life policies. Life insurance that covers a specified amount of time is called term life insurance. I would have liked to make everything so that I could cash it in at some point, but it is typically more expensive to get whole life policies than it is to get term life policies. Evaluate your financial situation and see what will work best for you.

9. **IRA/retirement fund**: You have to plan for retirement. I am not making this into some political thing where I make you panic that Social Security will not be around when it's time to retire. Nope. I run screaming from any political discussions. I find that they make me feel like my brain is about to melt and then someone always ends up crying. It's kind of like trying to teach your toddler quantum physics. But I digress. Social Security is a thing, but it will not allow you to live comfortably when you decide to retire. Every time I get one of those updates that tells me how much I will get monthly from social security in the future, I just laugh. I'm like, "with inflation, that should be about enough to buy rice and beans by the time I retire." So, let's talk about the two different types of IRAs. There are OTHER types if you own your own business or can afford to max out your IRA every year, but I don't know anyone who is like, "I just have so much money that I want to stuff it all into my IRA (s)!" If the average American doesn't have $1,000 in savings, I don't know how they are thinking about maxing out their IRA (s). So, read up a bit about IRAs, and decide what is best for you. Here are the basics:

   a. **There are traditional IRAs and Roth IRAs.** The main difference between a traditional IRA and a Roth IRA is that all of the money that you put into a traditional IRA during the year is tax-deductible on both state and federal tax returns during the year that you make the contribution. Before you get super excited and say, "yes! Put all my money in the traditional IRA!" know that when you retire and go to make withdrawals, those withdrawals are taxed at ordinary income tax rates. **Roth IRAs** don't give you any tax break when you put money in, but they are usually tax free when you take the money out after retirement. So you need to consider what will fit with your financial situation. Remember, there are some other types of IRAs if you have your own business or crazy amounts of money, so you can look into those. What do I have? I have both! I thought it was important for me personally to be able to have some tax deductions every year, but also to be able to have an account that won't be taxed when I retire. I do very strongly advise that you talk to a financial planner, and not just someone who makes commission on what you purchase. You might think that you are meeting with a financial planner when you sit down to open a IRA, but those people are mostly not objective because they work on commission. It will cost you a little money to work with someone who doesn't get commission, but you probably want to do that at least once before you make some big purchases. For the record, I didn't do that, but I just read my ass off, so I knew exactly what I wanted and needed when I went to open my retirement accounts. Most people do not have the patience to do that, however, so then it might just be worth it to pay for an hour consultation and bring all of your paystubs and other financial information. The good news is that, if you are starting early, no matter what type of IRA you open, you can make lots of money by just investing a little every month. If you are starting later, you are probably going to have to stretch a little to make enough to retire with. Just facts, sorry. I just want you to be prepared.

10. **Stocks/Other Investments**: So my dad did well by investing in real estate in the 80s. I wanted to do the same as an adult, and asked him for his help. I was surprised when he was against basically every single real estate investment that I (or my husband) came up with. Owning your own home is obviously something of an investment, but in terms of making additional investments, it usually takes A LOT of capital and can be very risky. You also really need to know what you are doing, hire lawyers, be good with paperwork, take out landlord's insurance (if you plan on renting the property), deal with any heating/plumbing/electrical issues that come up and OMG do you have a headache yet? Real Estate tends to have big risks and big rewards, but who needs all of that extra stress, seriously? So I decided to do some smaller investments in stocks, but I have been very successful. I am successful because I mix some "blue chip" stocks with some pharmaceutical stocks and then some newer companies, so that everything is diversified. I don't' know how to "play the stock market" or do anything like that. For me, these have been investments that I went into with a long-term mindset. Stocks are also nice because you don't have to wait until retirement to cash them. A few years back, some unexpected bills came up, and I cashed some stocks to pay them. You can't do that with an IRA or Whole Life Policy without paying crazy penalties. You also can't make a property that you bought liquid in just a few weeks. So, I am a fan of using stocks as a long-term investment that you can liquefy over the short term if necessary. You have to decide what works best for you and what your budget is for stocks. I don't invest in stocks regularly, honestly. With all of my regular, steady investments, I don't always have the extra Benjamins floating around to do that. So, I just put money into my stock account when I have it, and then I have a list of stocks that I want to purchase. I also have some index funds (which are mixes of stocks that are designed to mimic the DOW). I do lots of research on all of these stocks. It's really easy to see how they have performed over the last several days, weeks, months, and years in the "research" section of my TD Ameritrade account. For my son, we chose a Fidelity

account that also allows us the luxury of lots of research. Do some HOMEWORK (notice a theme here? Everyone's situation is different so you need to do what will fit your life). See what you are most comfortable doing. This chapter might seem a little overwhelming at first, but just by doing one thing at a time, you will be shocked at how much you are able to accumulate in ten years.

4 WAIT, I'M SUPPOSED TO BE NICE?

Before I get into how to make your relationships sparkly and nice, I would advise absolutely everyone to read *The Relationship Protocol*. I have nothing to gain from referring you to this book. I have never even met the author. What I can tell you is that it saved my marriage and has profoundly affected all of my relationships. It has also helped me to build better relationships when I meet new people. Debra Roberts (the author) shows you how to build better relationships using some simple steps and gives lots of great examples.

Have you read it yet? NO? Go read it. In the meantime, I am going to just give you some basics

1. **Giving to others and loving others unconditionally benefits both parties**: I think that Americans generally place a little bit too much emphasis on "what's in this relationship for me?" Since we tend to have that attitude, when we are asked to do things for others, we feel "put upon" or like we aren't getting what we need. Sometimes, the reason why we aren't getting what we need is simply because we are not putting enough in. If you want to grow a plant, you have to water it. If you want your dog to be happy and to think you are a God, you have to give him food, water, cuddles, and walks. So why would you think it is any different with your friends or your romantic relationships? If I tell my husband I love him every day and do nice little things for him like send him notes, drop off and pick up his dry-cleaning, pick up his favorite coffee drink while I am out running errands, or make him tacos when we both get home late and nobody feels like cooking, several wonderful things happen:

a. I feel good because I am making the person I love happy.
b. He feels good because he knows that I am thinking of him.
c. Finally, if I need to ask a favor of him (like bathing the dogs or something that would otherwise be difficult for me to do), he might not be really excited about doing it, but he will do his best.

Think about the alternative. If I constantly ask my husband for money, to fix things around the house, or to run errands for me, I will become a "nag" in no time flat. Do you know anyone who likes being called a nag? I didn't think so. Show your love in little ways. Stop thinking it's all about you.

2. **Open mouth, insert foot? You can avoid that:** In the heat of an argument, it can be very easy to say some nasty things. I mean, really nasty things. It's stuff that you might not actually mean, but you can bet that the other person will have a hard time forgiving some of that. Can you blame them? So here it goes: "stop saying dumb shit." Usually, right before you say something that will put your relationship in a terrible place for several weeks, there is a period of escalation. You start to feel that vein in your neck throbbing, or you feel like Bruce Banner right before he becomes the Incredible Hulk. You know the signs. You're about to start throwing stuff (either verbally or literally: either way it isn't good). What you need to do at that point is slow things down and think. This can be hard, especially if you are in a situation where you are trying to prove yourself right. Think a little about the other person's perspective. Does *any* of what he or she is saying make sense? Is there at least a small point or two that you can agree on? You can often use that small point as a start and then work your way back into civil conversation via one small agreement. It sounds simple, but it's a start.

I also want you to take notice of your tone, since this can be very important for both parties involved. Is your tone escalating? This is a huge problem with many fights and only ever makes things worse: you hear the words, which might be rational, but because of HOW the words are said, you are reacting to HOW things are said as opposed to WHAT is said. It seems simple enough to differentiate, but it is really difficult at times. So it is sometimes helpful, while arguing, to remind each other to keep the tones civil so that you can focus on the CONTENT and come to a resolution that way.

One other thing that you want to consider is if there have been events preceding the current disagreement that might make you more snippy with that person or even more prone to pick a fight. Is this something that has been building over time and you are just now seeing it come to a head? If so, how can we separate that out and work with it in a constructive way? Are you bringing your own baggage to the table? Are you at a point when your hormones are crazy or when your dog is sick or your mom just gave you the business about something that you thought was stupid? This seems silly, but those things can really affect your interactions with everyone. The energy you bring to any conversation will permeate that conversation, even if you don't mean for it to do so. That's why, after you have just had a fight with your mortgage company because they are idiots and can never get anything right (you must have Bank of America too!), you then jump down your spouse's throat for leaving his sweaty, horrid socks someplace other than the laundry basket. You tell him that he should just throw them in the garbage (yes, they are really that bad). Then he takes your bad energy and throws it back at you because he has had a rough day. Before you know it, things pretty much devolve into something that kind of resembles ping pong. But with turds. And nobody likes that. I mean, I don't think anybody likes that. So you can stop this poopy ping pong by not coming to the conversation with all of that other baggage. Even do a little Tai Chi, yoga, or some grounding to make sure you get all of the emotional gunk off of you before you end up inadvertently throwing it all over someone else. Hell, try smudging, it worked for the Native Americans. You simply can't expect sunshine and rainbows from the other party, if you are all Voldemort and cockroaches. I mean, it just doesn't make sense. Tell the other person you care. Tell them you need a break from the conversation because it is getting too intense. And for heaven's sake, once again, watch your TONE! I cannot tell you how many problems begin because one party just starts out immediately sounding irritated or otherwise imposed upon. That is no way to do business. If you see your tone getting all wacko, apologize, and ask to start over. Bad tone can put the other party or parties on the defensive right away. Before you ask for something or address a sensitive topic, think of the best way to do it (aka, the way that will take the other party's feelings into consideration and leave the lines of communication open). Just keep in mind that in this digital age, there are so many methods of communication *other* than speaking in person. This can be challenging because seeing your hand gestures, facial expressions, and hearing your inflection are all part of the whole communication experience. That's often why written communication can easy get misconstrued or misinterpreted. Think about it: text, email, Facebook posts, and even Twitter posts tend to get people into loads of trouble, so don't take these mediums for granted, especially when trying to communicate something important. Very recently, I felt like a conversation was escalating through TEXT! I was starting to feel put out and like the other person was not taking responsibility and I could definitely feel frustration and tension on the other side too. So I waited a long, long time to respond and thought about lots of different scenarios in my head. I waited until I cooled down mentally. And you know what? Everything is Gucci. If I had just reacted the way I intended to react originally, though, I am sure it would have turned into a fight and hurt feelings. Isn't it nice to know that you can avoid that type of stuff?

3. **Build Trust (show you deserve it):** I have definitely noticed that a very common problem in relationships is trust. For many people, I think that they link trust to fidelity, but that is just one small portion. Trust can be a huge issue in a relationship between a parent and a teenager if that teenager has snuck out of the house or been caught stealing something. With a married couple, the way that money is spent can be a huge trust issue. If hubby wants to save to buy a nice home and wifey keeps spending money on designer shoes, that can be a trust issue too. Personally, I would side with hubby on that one, since who the heck cares if you have designer shoes? Trust really means that you can be relied upon to do what you say you are going to do. So trust might be implied in a friendship or in a marriage, but when you keep saying you will do things that you don't do (even if they SEEM like small things), you are destroying the trust component in that relationship. For example, I had a friend who would constantly say something like this, "are you free the weekend of the 21st? Because I would llloovvvvee to see you then. Let's make plans!" So we would make plans, and then something would *always* come up for her (unless she really needed some kind of emotional support: then she would magically appear as if she had apparated). I think you get where I am going with this. After this happened again and again and again, I stopped considering her my friend, because that is just not a considerate thing to do. Even though it is a small issue of trust, it became increasingly important after a while. So do this: whether you are a friend, a son, a mother, a brother, a spouse, or an employee, EARN trust in your relationships. If you have been a dolt in the past, you are going to have to work a bit harder. If you are in ANY kind of relationship with someone whom you don't trust, ask yourself WHY you are in that relationship. Is this something that can be ameliorated, or has this been going on for years with little hope of resolution? If it is the latter, then you need to seriously evaluate the relationship,

because, in my estimation, all good relationships are built on trust.

4. **The Common Values:** Okay, you will never share EVERY value in common with everyone, nor should you. The world has tons of fun, debatable gray areas, and you might even be inclined to be friends with people who challenge your viewpoints because you like that challenge. If so, good for you!!!! Way to expand your horizons! On the other hand, there are some relationships that can be absolutely doomed. A vegan and a hunter, for example? Yeah, that's not gonna work. I have AMAZING neighbors who are all about Jesus and living His word and helping others and raising children in God's name. They have open hearts and open minds and I am so grateful to live next to such amazing people. They have a strong, wonderful marriage and two beautiful boys. They do not argue with each other. Ever. It's all about the love. It is wonderful to see. Why is their relationship so perfect? Much of it has to do with the fact that they are such amazing people individually, but another part of it is their shared value system. Your shared value system certainly doesn't have to be religion. Since I think that lots of different religions are beautiful, I can appreciate when people show enthusiasm about them. I find that as I get older, though, I can't be around people who like to place blame on others, or make excuses, or complain all of the time. For me, people who do this do not share my value system. I also have difficulty with people who give me the "Yes, but…" response to positive stories. This shit drives me crazy. "Yes, but she had so much support around her," or "Yes, but she has a job that is always in demand." Ugh. Stop making up reasons why you can't succeed. Suck it up! If you are a person who values hard work and constant self-improvement, you are just not going to have good long-term relationships with people who are slovenly, lazy pigs. That is not going to work. If you are really into saving the environment, you probably won't do really well with people who think that climate change isn't a thing. Just saying. Strong relationships have strong

backbones, so be realistic. There are going to be people whom you are going to only spend short periods of time with, and you don't have to have any kind of profound relationship. If that's the case and you have really different values, then no biggie. I mean, you can probably fake it and avoid talking about politics for a night or two every once in a while (hell, I try to spend a lifetime avoiding this subject!), but the people whom you are really close with? You need to find at least a few shared values, so that you can keep the relationship stable. For example, if your sister wants to become a follower of Krishna and give up all her earthly possessions, and you want to work towards buying a mansion in Beverly Hills with illicitly obtained funds, then you guys are probably going to have some things that you don't totally see eye-to-eye on. That's okay, because you might both be really passionate about helping to feed the hungry and you might love to talk about hockey. Or you might both really love to cook and do things to help your parents. Basically, it comes down to this: for the people who are going to be a huge part of your life, it is best to make sure that you have at least SOME shared values. For the family that you were born into, you might have to dig to find those values, but use that as the glue that holds the relationships together and stop arguing over nonsense.

5. **Be Honest. No really**: Don't skip this section!! People tend to think that this doesn't apply to them, because they are always totally honest in their relationships. Right. Let's take a minute to examine that. When was the last time that you told your partner or your parent that you were going someplace different than you were actually going? When was the last time that you purposefully hid something from someone you are in a relationship with for fear of how that person might react? AH-HA!!!! You are busted. I am not doing this so that we can examine all of the ways in which you are a terrible person. I think that this is something that we don't even really think about. I am officially the world's worst liar. I mean, the worst. I have to tell the truth. But I know that most people see no

harm in a little deception (or some white lies) here and there. When it comes to the people whom you are closest to, this is a very bad idea, and should be avoided. For example, if you have been talking to that hot girl (or guy) from work whom you know is single, and things seem a little flirty, a lot of people would just prefer not to mention something like that to a spouse. C'mon now! Your spouse is your support system and will help you to avoid doing some dumb, dumb stuff that could seriously wreck your whole life. I mean it. There was once someone whom I was writing back and forth with about sports and he seemed to be suggesting we go out for drinks. Guess who the first person I told was? My husband. He didn't freak out or get upset. He definitely appreciated me telling him. Right away, he was just like, okay, so we can all go out for drinks together then! Okay!! Good idea! No chance for anything to get weird or out-of-control that way. See? That was easy. No one has to get upset or do anything deceptive. Problem solved.

There are certainly other ways that people can be dishonest with each other, though. Some people hide debt or other significant expenditures from their spouses. What are you doing??? That person is going to be so much more upset when they find out that you are keeping this debt a secret!! You are making a huge mistake. Yes, rational people think that my husband and I occasionally "overshare" with one another. I think most people probably feel the same way about the relationship that I have with my parents (hell, sometimes *I* feel that way!), but what I get in exchange for that is a kind of trust that I will never take for granted. Yes, we are mortal and argue and get annoyed over dumb stuff, but is there anyone in the world that I trust more than my parents? NO way. And that's all built on all honesty, all the time. It's the only way to go. Take baby steps with this at first if you have to, but trust is probably the most valuable resource in your life.

6. **Stop saying mean things about other people:** I am not going to lie, this is a hard one. This is a rule that I break

myself sometimes, particularly when I feel that people have dug themselves into their own mess and then want others to help them out. Also, let's face it: people can be annoying, cruel, make dumb decisions, and generally mess up their lives willy nilly (maybe just get them a copy of this book ;)). Soooo, we want to make sure that we are part of the solution as opposed to perpetuating the problem. My family and I used to have an inside joke if we would criticize someone (which is something that we happen to do a lot to each other, by the way). We would sigh heavily and say something to the effect of, "being perfect is so hard." This is comedic gold because, of course, no one is perfect, but we all tend to judge others as if we are. Take a second, have some compassion, and try to see things from the other person's perspective. There are going to be some people whom you simply can't do this for. I understand. We are all a work in progress. Then just try not to spend time with those people so that you don't end up talking shit about them behind their backs. A while ago, I would often get in the habit of complaining to others about things that my husband did. Though this isn't the same as calling him a twit or a d-bag or some other nasty thing, it still creates negative energy in your relationship and complaining about your spouse does not hold you in good esteem with the person you are speaking to. It also forces YOU to only think about the negative things that your spouse does instead of focusing on the positive. So I have created a little exercise for myself. If I am about to think or say something negative about my husband, I try to cancel it out with something positive. For example, if I am about to complain about how he never closes the drawers or is always on his phone, I then try to instead focus on how good he is at giving hugs, or how much he cares about humanity as a whole. One thing that we tend to personally fight over is my husband's tendency to help anyone any amount. For example, he will offer his assets to people who request them, even if those people ask time and time again or, in my estimation, are undeserving of them. This kind of drives me a little crazy sometimes. But then I have to say to myself how he does this because he is such a profoundly good person and wants to help everyone. I just don't want him getting taken advantage of!!! So, it isn't always easy to be nice, but switching the way that YOU think is often the key (as opposed to trying to make the other person change.

7. **Stop Complaining About Everything:** What does it feel like to be around someone who complains about everything all of the time? I mean, it kind of feels like you are being hit over the head with a wet fish repeatedly. Positive, well-meaning people are not going to want to hang out with anyone who is constantly complaining. That's because positive people want to remain positive. They didn't get that way by injecting rainbows every morning. One day, they just made a conscious decision to stay positive. That means that if you are constantly bitching and moaning, the only other people that you will attract into your life will be the ones who also like to bitch and moan. I mean, is that really what you want? Do you want one of those little Charlie Brown clouds around your life at all times, so that when good people see you coming they're like, "Don't make eye contact. Don't make eye contact!"? Do you have trouble staying positive? I get that. If you watch the news, you would think that the world is disintegrating into a big pile of manure on a daily basis. Do yourself a favor and don't watch the news unless you are trying to get depressed, in which case, knock yourself out. Stop watching those political shows that blame everything on the other party. Blame is nothing but deciding not to take personal responsibility. Defriend all of the people on Facebook who are constantly spreading doom and gloom on social media. I am serious. If you start seeing the world without your glasses covered in poop, you will not only be happier and more grateful, but you will start attracting more positive things into your life. Even if the fictional television that you watch is really dark (let's just say, for example, that the only thing that you watch is *Game of Thrones*), you are going to see the world through some weird, incestuous lenses.

My husband is a big believer in not reading any Stephen King because he feels that there is a lot of negative energy in that fiction. This is very good logic to me.

When you are on a diet of positivity, you will find that your whole life seems better. Once you start seeing positive, happy things in your social media, stop watching the shit parade that is the news, and watch only programming that either makes you laugh or makes you think, you will start feeling more positive in general, and that will start manifesting as positivity in your relationships. I would also recommend that you stop watching commercials. Commercials are essentially made to make you want to purchase things that you don't, in all probability, need. The commercials for pharmaceuticals are basically designed to make you think that you have some sort of nefarious disease so that you will go to your doctor and ask for exactly what you saw on television. Ugh. You would be surprised how much less junk you want if you stop watching dumb advertisements that try to tell you what you want. Instead, enumerate the things that you are grateful for. Gratitude goes a long way in terms of making you happier, healthier, and improving your relationships.

8. **Cut off the ties that are dragging you down:** This is a hard one, I know. That person who was your best friend in college but is now addicted to prescription painkillers and is always asking you to bail her out of situations that she shouldn't be in to begin with? Yeah, stop hanging out with her. Maybe that will be the wakeup call that she needs. The person who only ever calls you when they want something? That's a relationship that you might want to reconsider too. The person who is always talking smack about others? You get the idea. You are like the people you surround yourself with, so if you are looking at some of those people and they do not reflect your best self, be compassionate, but consider whether or not that relationship is worth it for you.

Simply put, most of the time, the biggest issues in relationships are communication, trust, and respect. Look at the relationships that you have that are struggling and try to evaluate WHY they are struggling. I don't believe that you can love someone madly and then one day you suddenly hate that person. Either communication broke down, one of you has grown tremendously as a person and the other hasn't, or there were problems to begin with that you ignored. Therapy is a very under-utilized tool. Don't mistake a rough patch in a relationship for the end of a relationship and always express love and gratitude to the people whom you care about so that they may thrive and grow. In that way, you are creating more love, light, and positivity in the world. You are also enabling others to become their highest selves through you. Doesn't that feel nice????

5 WHY IT'S SO EASY TO BE FAT AND SICK

I am going to be completely honest here. The only reason that you can't find any fat pictures of me on the internet are because I have a team of well-trained assassins who "take out" anyone who might potentially have fat pictures of me.

Oh no wait, that's not it.

It's a little less interesting than all of that. The Internet was kind of still in toddlerhood when I was in college and so there wasn't a whole lot of posting going on.

Hence, not a lot of fat pics.

However, just to put things in perspective, I am seven months pregnant as I write this and I am still just shy of my college weight during my senior year.

So I don't want any of you haters out there telling me that I am slender because I have good genetics or that I have had a very healthy pregnancy at age 37 because I am lucky.

That is a bunch of horseshit, seriously.

Like most Americans, I spent most of my life with my weight yo-yoing dramatically. In my late twenties, my bloodwork was always a mess (to the point where several doctors actually encouraged me to get a bone marrow biopsy, which I grudgingly did). I was always tired (I actually had almost all of the symptoms of narcolepsy), I was always having joint pain, constant congestion, and constant injury. I can remember getting a phone call from my primary care doctor one day asking me to come in as soon as possible. Scared, I went that day. She basically sat me down to tell me in person that, if my bloodwork and hormone levels continued as they were, I would probably have trouble conceiving. Thank God, I had no plans on conceiving anytime in my twenties. In fact, I didn't think I wanted to have biological children at all until, oh, about 7 months ago lol.

So am I incredibly grateful for where I am in life right now? You can't even imagine. Sometimes, just thinking about all of the wonderful people in my life, thinking about the things I have done, and thinking about the beautiful baby inside me, I just get totally overcome with emotion and gratitude.

But none of it has anything to do with luck at all. Things could have very easily gone the other way from a standpoint of health and weight (and yes, the two are inextricably linked). So let me save you all of the time and research that I did, so that you can start to see results right away. Here are some things that can dramatically affect your weight and health:

1. Food sensitivities
2. Hormone or immune regulation disruption (this can be cause by things found in deodorant, perfumes, meat, abrasive cleaners, pesticides, plastics, things that off-gas, etc.)
3. The people whom you spend the most time with
4. Your ability to use portion control (no really!!! There is no magic trick, you need to learn portion control)
5. Your exercise routine
6. Having the right micronutrients on board to control food cravings and make your body function optimally.
7. Emotional associations with eating

Okay, so if you have read *Unleash Your True Athletic Potential*, you already know about food sensitivities, but basically, here it is: because contemporary foods have been so far removed from their original form, many people have difficulty processing them, which affects the way the body regulates other chemical processes. It's not surprising then, that the foods that have been the most tampered with from the standpoint of genetic modification are the ones that tend to give people the most trouble, namely:

- Corn
- Wheat
- Soy
- Peanuts
- Dairy

There are several reasons why many people have difficulty losing weight or even feeling good when eating animal products. These products can cause severe health outcomes over the long-term when eaten in large quantities. When all of my bloodwork was a hot mess, for example, I was eating what would be considered a very healthy diet by most standards. Lots of fish, dairy, whole grains, yogurt and vegetables. But here are some reasons why you want to skip the animal products as often as is possible (this section was written with the help of Dr. Robert Ostfeld)

1. **Eating animal products is strongly associated with heart disease**: Most people already know that eating meat introduces cholesterol into the body. What many people don't know is that when meat is consumed, the body forms TMAO (trimethylamine-N-oxide). TMAO is associated with plaque building up in the arteries (atherosclerosis) and higher levels of TMAO in the blood are associated with worse heart outcomes. For those of you who think that milk "does a body good," the choline in milk also breaks down into TMAO. Those embracing a plant-based diet produce virtually no TMAO. Those who eat a plant-based diet also have less of the gut bacteria that "help" form TMAO.

    Another threat to the arteries lies in foam cells. Foam cells may live in the walls of the arteries, contributing to atherosclerosis. Green leafy vegetables produce nitric oxide in the blood. Nitric oxide helps to destroy foam cells and dilate blood vessels. Eating leafy green vegetables also increases endothelial regenerative cells: important cells that make up the walls of the blood vessels. I think that you can easily see how eating mostly fruits and vegetables is the best thing for your heart health.

2. **Eating animal products increases your risk of obesity**: Fruits, vegetables, and beans are the staples of a plant-based diet and are naturally low in calories. These foods are also very high in fiber, making it difficult to overeat them. On the other hand, meats, dairy, and processed foods are very calorically dense. A 2009 study exploring the relationship between high- and low-energy dense diets, satiety, and obesity proved that individuals eating these calorically dense foods ate up to twice as many calories in a day in order to achieve satiety. Since fruits and vegetables are also far more nutrient-dense than animal products, individuals following a plant-based diet get more vitamins, minerals, antioxidant protection, and a host of other phytochemicals.

3. **Eating animal products can increase muscle soreness**: My husband always likes to brag about how he completed the first marathon of his life just a few weeks after his 40th birthday thanks to a vegan diet. He feels that he never would have been able to recover as quickly or fuel as well if he were eating the animal foods that generate so much inflammation and are so much harder for your body to break down. He's probably right: good nutrition plays a major role in the process of regenerating muscles after training and workouts. Eating lots of fruits and vegetables gives an athlete's body the building blocks it needs to create strong muscles and healthy bones. Plant foods also help to make the body very alkaline. An alkaline body is an enormous advantage in the healing process. When the body is acidic, it takes longer to recover. Processed foods, meat, and dairy can develop an acidic environment in the body. Over time, a constantly acidic body can lead to injury and compromised immunity.

4. **Plant-based diets help fight diabetes**: The tremendous increase in the number of diabetic individuals in the US has corresponded with increasing waistlines. A host of other health complications typically plague diabetics: they have a much higher incidence of heart attack, stroke and kidney damage. Dr. Joel Fuhrman and Dr. Milton Crane have observed decreases in peripheral neuropathy and, in the cases of Type II diabetics, a complete reversal of diabetes in patients for whom they prescribed a vegetable-rich plant-based diet.

5. **Plant-based diets decrease exposure to dangerous antibiotics/hormones**: Meat producers give growth hormones

and antibiotics to the animals intended to become food. When people consume these animals or products taken from these animals (such as cheese and other dairy products), they are exposed to these and other harmful toxins. Avoiding these products means avoiding substantial health risks.
6. **Plant-based diets may decrease allergies/asthma**: Casein, the protein found in milk, is known to trigger allergies. There has also been shown to be a correlation between TMAO and increased asthma attacks.
7. **Animal products can cause autoimmune flare-ups**: Most Americans get 2-3 times more protein than they actually need. When protein is burned, it leaves a nitrogen-containing residue in the form of ammonia. Ammonia is toxic and the body needs to get rid of it. This task taxes the liver, kidneys, and digestive system. Dr. Weil therefore advises individuals with autoimmune issues to adopt a lower-protein diet.
8. **Animal products are becoming increasingly linked with certain kinds of cancer**: Many substances that occur naturally in plant foods have been shown to be anti-carcinogenic. These substances do not work well as isolated compounds (meaning you can't just ingest them in pill form and receive the full spectrum of benefits), but rather, these substances work holistically when the plant is consumed. Allium compounds, catechins, ellagic acid, flavonoids, isoflavones, phenolic acids, protease inhibitors, and sterols are just a few examples of the thousands of anti-carcinogenic compounds found in whole foods. You may have also read the International Agency for Research on Cancer has officially declared that processed meats are carcinogenic. This conclusion was reached after twenty-two experts from 10 countries reviewed over 800 studies. Eating even the equivalent of about one hot dog a day can increase the risk of certain cancers by as much as 18%. They also determined that there was an increased risk of several different types of cancers strictly from eating red meat.

For those interested in embracing or learning more about a plant-based lifestyle, the cardiac wellness program at Montefiore medical center is a great resource. It is directed by Dr. Robert Ostfeld. A Registered Dietician is also available for those involved in the program . Visit www.montefiore.org/cardiacwellnessprogram for more information.

So in addressing food sensitivities and some of the dangers of eating meat on a regular basis, we have already touched a bit upon things that can disrupt your hormones or your immune system. There are other things that can wreak havoc in that same area, however. Just as everyone will have different food sensitivities, different people will react differently to various environmental toxins, with some people having autoimmune reactions, some people having weight gain, and still others having no noticeable reactions at all. So before you stop wearing deodorant and washing your hair, let me give you some things that you can replace certain personal care products with so that you aren't taking any unnecessary risks.

In my case, about 6 months into being vegan, all of my bloodwork starting coming back much better, but it wasn't 100 percent yet, and I kept on reading to find out what else might be affecting how I was feeling. As it turns out, there are lots of horrific things in personal care products. Many of these things are actually illegal in Europe and Canada, but still legal in the US. Go figure that. So what are personal care products? Deodorants, perfumes, soaps, shampoos, toothpaste, hair dye, mouthwash, detergents, and so on. I used to have a borderline obsessive addiction with fragrances. Like, I wouldn't be able to walk by a fragrance store without its siren song luring me in. After I read about the formaldehyde and other chemicals that are typically in fancy fragrances, I stopped buying all of those fragrances (and started saving boatloads of money). I found two vegan brands of fragrances that I really like. One is called Kleanspa and the other is called Harvey Prince Organics. Pacifica also makes some nice fragrances and they are pretty inexpensive. With the exception of those brands, I don't buy any fragrances on a regular basis. I would recommend buying personal care products that are vegan or vegetarian (even if that's not your thing) because they tend to mostly have botanical ingredients (meaning: made from plants as opposed to chemicals). In my research on personal care products, I was surprised to find out that antiperspirants are stopping a very important function in your body when you use them. People need to sweat to eliminate toxins and help cool themselves off. Sweating is good!!! Thus has begun a very long quest for a deodorant that is totally natural and actually works. I am just going to lay it out for you straight: most natural deodorants do not work. After about two hours, you smell like you made out with Chewbacca at Warped Tour in 90 degree heat. Seriously. I am therefore not going to subject you to being "the smelly kid" (even if you are an adult). A friend of mine had recommended Schmidt's deodorants when I told her of my Chewbacca woes, and, not expecting much, I bought some. This stuff is brilliant. It works all day and actually smells REALLY good. As far as body washes, shampoos, toothpaste, and so on, the stuff that you get at Whole Foods or Trader Joe's tends to be pretty good in terms of not housing too many scary chemicals. You might want to look at this list from the American Cancer Society, though, and see if some of the products you have contain any known carcinogens or potential carcinogens: https://www.cancer.org/cancer/cancer-causes/general-info/known-and-probable-human-carcinogens.html

That is also a good list to use when deciding which cleaners to use and which to avoid. Here is another list of often-used chemicals that you should try to avoid: https://www.naturalnews.com/038604_phthalates_cosmetics_hormone_disruption.html

I honestly just always use either Trader Joe's cleaning spray, baking soda and vinegar, or the Method Brand. I find I don't have any negative reactions to them. I also like the Attitude brand of products (partilcularly their stain remover spray). It is very easy to substitute natural products for the chemical stuff in most cases. In case of dryer sheets, though, that is not the case. Natural dryer sheets really suck: regardless of what brand you are trying. It's pretty much guaranteed that your clothes will come out like a static experiment and that you will shock everyone who comes within 5 feet of you. For this reason, I like dryer spray instead. It still probably doesn't work as well as the conventional stuff for static, but it suffices as long as everything you own is not made of polyester.

Also of note, polyester and synthetic fabrics can off-gas. That doesn't mean I don't use them, because I do, but I would never buy a new comforter or a new set of pillows or a mattress with polyester fill. That essentially means that you are breathing in all of that off-gassing. And if your bedroom is anything like my bedroom at night, between two dogs and two humans, there is already a ton of off-gassing going on.

But I digress.

Other things that can off-gas and affect your hormones are paints, particle board furniture, furniture finish, and the pans you cook with. When we were preparing the bedroom for our former foster children, we used the most natural paint possible, an organic mattress, sheets, and a crib with absolutely no lacquer (from IKEA, actually). Even if the things that you use for yourself aren't free of harmful chemicals, children, with their developing immune systems, should have limited exposure to off-gassing (insert more fart jokes here). We have used cast iron pans for so long (thanks to my husband) that I completely even forgot that people cook with things others than cast iron. Those no-stick pans? Totally bad news. A recent study found that using them can actually make weight loss more difficult. Teflon is an industrial surface coating that really shouldn't be anywhere near what you eat. Perfluorooctanoic acids are toxic and released whenever those non-stick pans are overheated. My husband, the pharmacist, says long-term use can create neurological damage. He is smart. Stay away from this stuff. Use only cast iron or uncoated stainless steel. Coat your pans in olive oil and clean them. Trust me, a little extra time cleaning every day is worth not leaking poisons into your body.

Speaking of avoiding leaking poisons into your body…..

The people whom you spend the most time with impact your health and waistline. Believe it or not, the best indicator of whether or not you will be overweight is if the people whom you spend the most time with are overweight. Their eating habits become yours (even if those eating habits are terrible). Also, if they smoke, drink, or do drugs, you are much more likely to think that these things are normal or okay. If your friends stress you out or make lots of bad decisions, you are generally going to feel like that is the state of the world, and chaos ensues. So choose your friends and acquaintances wisely, because that is where you are also choosing whom to be influenced by.

The other element involved in health and a slim waistline that is not particularly popular right now is the idea of portion control. I think that it doesn't get a lot of love because people perceive it to be hard. I'm not sure why. Do you think that it's easy to eat bacon-wrapped shrimp and pork rinds for every meal? That is absurdity. That stuff is killing you. That is why I absolutely love my portion containers. You can order them here:

https://www.teambeachbody.com/shop/d/beachbody-portion-control-7-piece-container-kit-BBPortionControlContainer?referringRepID=1398383

They come with a little book to let you know exactly how many containers you should have every day. This is based on your own unique goals, which is really important. Someone who is trying to gain muscle should not be eating the same way as someone who wants to slim down. The magic diet fairies do not simply adapt to your wants. You have to do a little bit of math. Don't be scared. It only requires that you do math once (win!). Just from doing this ONE time, you can have a formula to use on and on indefinitely (unless your fitness goals change). It makes something that was once so hard so much easier. I was in very good shape when I was just eating a vegan diet that was low in sugar. Once I started using the containers, though, my body got ripped up. I mean, I was amazed at how much it changed. And the portions have been a blessing throughout my pregnancy because it makes it easier for me to make sure that BOTH baby and I have the right amount of nutrition. I don't care what dietary approach you subscribe to, you can never eat as much of ANYTHING as you would like (except maybe spinach, and nobody really wants to do that). Do yourself a favor and learn to use portion control. It seems like a lot of work at first, but you can take the containers out to eat with you and then bag the rest. Eventually, you will find it to be really liberating because you don't have to count calories or use only pre-made frozen meals that make you a social pariah. Plus, then you look in the mirror after a few months and think, "so this is what it feels like to be totally awesome."

Your exercise routine also has a lot to do with your health (and not just how you look). Exercising improves your cardiovascular system, your metabolism, your mood, and a host of other things. The key is that you have to find an exercise that you will like enough to get you going. I personally love the Beachbody workouts, but what I would actually like even more if it were a possibility is swimming. I completely love swimming. I swear I was a dolphin in another life. I don't swim fast, though. I don't know if I would enjoy it as much if I did. Which brings me to my next point: you have to adjust to your ability level. I find that the reason why a lot of people hate exercising so much is because they will go through a period of time when they do absolutely nothing and then one morning wake up and say, "today I will run three miles." The next day, they can't walk, and the cycle repeats itself.

So, think of some activities that involve movement that you like, and start at YOUR skill level. With Beachbody, some nice beginner programs are You V. 2, Three Week Yoga Retreat, and Country Heat. Once you do well with those programs, you can move on to some intermediate programs like Shift Shop (but modified) then you can do the advanced stuff like P90X or Insanity. That progression should take a long time. Don't try to jump right to the front. If you can't see yourself doing any of the awesome Beachbody programs in your house, then just think of some things you like to do that require moving. Think along the following lines:

Ice skating
Hiking
Skiing
Swimming
Martial Arts

Obstacle Fitness (like climbing through trees to a zipline or climbing walls, etc.)
Any kind of sport
Yoga

If you are just starting out getting back into the world of fitness, you have to make it fun at first. Make the activity itself rewarding as opposed to making the reward about how your body will look. Not everyone enjoys going to the gym. Some people love fitness with a buddy, but others would prefer to work out on their own. What category do you fall under? If you need a friend, invite someone over for a workout and shakeology after. Or make plans to go on a hike together. Or join a karate class together (just make sure that it meets more than once a week, otherwise it won't do you much good). If you like to be a lone wolf, running is sometimes great for clearing your mind. I had an awesome guidance counselor in middle school who used to run during her lunch break every day. I always thought that was so cool. You can do something similar, but just keep in mind that working out first thing in the morning is pretty much always better because you don't have a million other things vying for your attention. Later in the day, more demands are often put on you, but if you can make arrangements to meet at the same time every day with a friend, and that friend is someone whom you really enjoy spending time with, then that will really go a long way towards getting you to do what you need to do.

So now you are working out and using portion control. These are things that will help you to lose weight, but how can you *feel* good? Eating *well* (meaning mostly organic foods with lots of fruits and vegetables) has even more to do with how you look and feel than what kind of cardio you are doing. When you eat lots of crap and processed foods, you aren't getting a lot of vitamins and minerals, so you feel hungry all of the time. I felt like most of my life I just couldn't stop feeling hungry. After doing tons of research, I realized that this was because I was eating lots of overly processed foods, and pretty much none of it was organic. This is a recipe for disaster. Part of the reason that your body will signal hunger cues (even sometimes right after you just ate) is because, although you may been eating a lot of calories, if those calories do not contain a lot of micronutrients, then your body is not getting what it needs out of the food, and you will consequently have lots of cravings. You could easily eat 500 calories in fast food and get essentially no nutrition at all, but if you ate 500 calories in fruits and vegetables, you would have a hard time trying to eat a whole lot more after that. Why? In addition to the tremendous amount of water and fiber in fruits and veggies, they are tremendous sources of micronutrients (the vitamins, minerals, antioxidants, and other amazing compounds that your body needs to function properly). If you are thinking: "but I take a multivitamin!" It is not the same, since many of these are created synthetically so they are not quite utilized by your body in the same way. I go into much more detail regarding this in *Unleash Your True Athletic Potential*, but suffice it to say that your best source of nutrition is food. That's another reason why I love Shakeology. It's made from real superfoods (foods that are naturally very high in vitamins and minerals), which is why it is so satisfying.

Okay, so now let's talk about the elephant in the room: the thing that can keep you from losing weight even if you do everything else right: your emotional associations with eating. I once heard someone say that the reason why there is a market for faux meats and vegan meats is because people naturally crave meat. Okay, that is entirely false. The truth though, is that we have lots of emotional associations with eating meat from our childhood, so we often find faux meats comforting. Children who grew up vegetarian or vegan often think that faux meat tastes really weird. Take a moment and try to list some foods that you KNOW you have emotional associations with. Do it now, and it will probably help you to understand a lot more about your own eating habits. What are some foods that often came up in your childhood for good occasions or bad occasions? How do you feel about those foods now?

I will give you an example. My parents generally were good about not forcing my brother or I to eat a food that we refused, but once my mom made a meatloaf that she and my dad were both adamant that I eat. I could not leave the table until I ate a certain amount. I don't know if that meatloaf actually tasted bad or it just tasted bad to me, but I was totally repulsed by it and henceforth have not EVER eaten meatloaf. Obviously, at this point I have been vegan for nearly ten years, so I wouldn't eat it anyway, but TO THIS DAY the thought of it really grosses me out. Another instance from my childhood really colored the way I look at noodles. My brother used to like noodles with butter when he was little (I know: worst food combo ever, right?). I decided that I wanted to try it too, and I did and I liked it BUT then proceeded to decorate our kitchen with my body weight's equivalent in puke directly thereafter. So guess what I haven't eaten since?

In terms of positive childhood associations, though, I have some unique ones. A book that I used to love had a scene in it where the characters made a mushroom soup for a tawny, scrawny lion. My mom also always loved mushrooms, and since I thought that she was the coolest, I wanted to like mushrooms too. Honestly, I hated the way that mushrooms tasted the first several times that I tried them as a child. I remember choking them down because I had such positive emotional associations with them. Eventually, I grew to really like them, but it definitely wasn't innate. I *learned* to like mushrooms.

Do you have similar stories from your childhood? I can think of at least 2-3 more for both positive and negative associations. Follow your own stories and see where they lead you. Finally, explore whether or not food was used for reward or punishment in your household, since this can have a staggering impact on your adult life.

What do I mean by using food as reward or punishment?

Unfortunately, many parents are very well-meaning, but use food (especially treats) to reinforce certain behaviors and discourage others. One that I feel is particularly bad is telling a misbehaving child, "now you are going to bed without supper!" On the other hand, it is so easy to use food as a reward without thinking about how it will affect the child's future associations with food. After having our foster kids, I caught myself doing this too! It is very easy to give a child a cookie for doing well, but think about how, as an adult, this could be problematic. If you have a rough day at work, you might want to "reward" yourself with some ice cream because that is what you have learned. Just recognizing these associations can be very powerful, but then addressing them through therapy or hypnosis is even more powerful. Try to list a few circumstances where you were commonly rewarded or punished with food and try to extrapolate how that affects your relationship with food as an adult. This is NOT in any way about blaming your parents. Blaming never helps anyone. This is a way of figuring out things like: I was always forced to eat every ounce of broccoli on my plate, which is why I probably hate broccoli.

We are going to go a little bit more into associations you have with food, but also think about how food was modeled for you. My husband watched his mother do things like eating cake for breakfast and essentially eating herself into diabetes (really!). He could have modeled that behavior, but instead, he recognized that his life would consist of being miserable and sick all of the time if he didn't find a better way. So he tried several other ways until he found veganism, to which he credits his ability to run his first marathon after 40. I saw pretty healthy eating modeled my whole life and then just took it a step further as I got older.

Finally, recognize what foods you are connected to because they remind you of loved ones or create feelings of warmth and comfort. This is a very important exercise because it can help you to recognize when you eat not out of hunger, but when you eat because you need a hug or just someone to show you that they care. I have had a lot of food aversions since being pregnant, but this week, my husband went out and got me a tempeh marsala. Instantly, the taste and smell of the sauce made me think, "Grandma!" and ate more of that than I had eaten of anything in a very long time. We used to go to my grandma's house very often for holidays, and we always had a wonderful time, and this sauce tasted SO MUCH like the gravy she used to make. I probably would have eaten even more of it if there was more! This is a perfect example of how an emotional connection to a time and place (and an amazing person who is unfortunately no longer with us) really enhanced the flavor of the food and made it more of an *experience*. I would like you to think about some instances in which this might be the case for you. I have provided a list of foods, and I want you to think about how each of these foods could be associated with rewards, punishments, love, specific events, or other things having nothing to do with hunger (or even taste). Add to this list or make your own, and start to understand more about your emotional relationship with food.

Cake
BBQ
Hamburgers
Stuffing
Turkey
Glazed ham
Lettuce
Broccoli
Gingerbread men
Pasta
Cookies
Juice
Pie
Cheese

6 SPOILER ALERT: ENERGY ACTUALLY DOESN'T COME IN A CUP

I think we are all a little guilty of muttering the following phrase: "I just don't have any energy right now!" We have also somehow been conditioned to believe that the answer to our energy problems comes in the form of an "energy drink" that smells like turpentine and greatly increases the risk of having a stroke (seriously!). This chapter is going to focus on REAL energy.

Just to get a baseline, though, let's take a minute right now and write down some things that you associate with having lots of energy versus having low energy.

High energy:
1.
2.
3.

Low energy
1.
2.
3.

Did sleep, nutrition, or hydration make the first list? What about emotional well-being or a well-balanced schedule? What about spending time around people who really care about you or feed your creative spirit? It's okay, I'm not grading your answers: although you totally would have just gotten a big fat "F." Don't worry, I am going to make it so that you score an "A" the next time around. Let's get into discussing the things that affect your energy on a daily basis.

Sleep: Okay, you know you should be getting 7-8 hours a night and all, but this also has a lot of do with quality of sleep. If you are using electronics right before you go to bed, that can affect your quality of sleep. The same is true if your phone keeps going off all night with notifications and messages. Do you have a stalker? Yup, they are messing up your sleep cycle. Do you think that you have to answer every message and notification as soon as it comes in? You might be in an unhealthy, controlling relationship with your phone. Talk to your phone. Tell it you need some space. Your phone will understand. It is an inanimate object and can be left alone for 7-8 hours a night. You will see. It will be okay.

I know that some of you simply can't imagine taking off that electronic leash, but being randomly awoken during the night via the lights on your phone (even if the sound is off) may be something that you are not even cognizant of, but it will really affect your ability to get a restful night's sleep. It will therefore affect your energy levels the next day as well.

Along similar lines, do you know how sometimes you wake up in the middle of the night to void some water or put some more water in? If you turn on the light for that 4 am tinkle, that also messes up your sleep cycle. In general, any kind of artificial light can mess up your sleep cycle. This is why the experts who study sleep actually suggest having a nightlight in the bathroom or areas that you frequent when you awaken at the witching hour. For new nursing mothers, it is suggested that you sleep with a nightlight by the bed as long as it only emits a low light. It should be enough to see your baby by but not enough to bring you fully awake when you nurse. Makes sense, right?

Here is something else that may come as a surprise to you if you are not feeling generally well-rested: people who tend to stay up very late and then sleep much later the next day generally don't feel as energized as the people who go to bed early and get up early. Why? Daylight is an amazing thing. If you have trouble waking up in the morning (read: *me*), you will be amazed at how much better you feel if you wake up earlier and then expose yourself to sunlight first thing in the morning. People who try to live against daylight also tend to be weigh more than their daylight-loving counterparts. So do your best to adjust to getting up relatively early and getting to bed relatively early. I know that it's not easy to say, "no" to that extra episode of *Game of Thrones*, but trust me, that will not enhance your life in any appreciable way: especially when you are sacrificing sleep for it.

Exercise/Movement: What? This *again*? This exercise stuff must be really important if it is coming up so much. Yes: it *is* really important. Have you ever been on vacation tracking your steps on an app when you suddenly realize that you have walked several miles that day and you didn't even notice? In fact, you felt *better*? You had more energy! Yup. Remember that whole "an object in motion stays in motion unless acted upon by an outside force" thing? You need to be moving regularly to maintain good energy levels. If you are just sitting around all day , you are actually going to be way more tired. Unfortunately, most adults have days that consist of sitting at desks doing little other than typing at a computer. I am fortunate enough to have a profession that involves lots of movement all day. So I generally NEVER feel tired at work. Obviously, though, I have taken the time to sit down at a computer and write several books, and that involves some serious ass-in-chair time. So how do I deal with that? I have movement breaks. After an hour, I might walk the dogs, or get a snack, or stand up and do some light yoga. I might even take a break to do something different entirely, but it should all involve moving around to some degree. This also greatly decreases that sleepiness that you get while sitting at the computer. I don't know about you, but I have never ever fallen asleep running. I have, however, started to feel my eyes closing when writing for long periods of time (even though I am an awesome writer and I always write about super interesting things). So begin scheduling a little movement into every day: throughout the day. Don't even go an hour without moving in some way (unless you are sleeping, in which case you can totally be still if that is your thing: I know some of y'all thrash like the Tazmanian Devil).

Positive Mental Attitude/Your Peeps: Okay, developing a positive attitude can be work. I am not going to pretend that I was born a ball of sunshine, rainbows and unicorns. In fact, I went through a period where I really struggled with depression. For me, high school, parts of college, and my first year after college were huge struggles. Now that I look back on it, though, I realize that it was because I wasn't looking at things the way I should have been and then I flocked to people who looked at things in the same negative way. Does this sound familiar? So let's just look at some simple examples, so I can show you how to adjust your thinking in a way that can really benefit you.

Here's an example. Someone wanted to become a client and scheduled several weeks in advance. For the first lesson, they didn't show, but swore that "they weren't like that" and that they would pay me for the missed lesson and that it would never happen again. I prefer to give most people the benefit of the doubt initially, so I believed them, and though I gently reminded them that they owed me money from the first lesson after I saw them (and they still did not pay), I continued to allow them to schedule with me. Two lessons later, they canceled with less than two hours notice. Now initially, I was really annoyed. I have a cancellation policy that was ignored twice, and this meant that I was losing money but MORE IMPORTANTLY that my time was not being respected. Then I decided to do a little homework and found out that there were several other reasons why I would not want them as clients. So yes, I lost over $120 and I could dwell on that and get upset and then allow them to reschedule and make every attempt to chase my money down. I could have let this continue to stress me every time that they scheduled. Instead, I just decided to drop them as clients and am grateful that I am saving myself both scheduling difficulties and other difficulties in the future. I did not need that negative energy in my professional life. My clients are amazing. I love to see them every time I work with them. Why would I let one person ruin such a great thing? Not a chance. I looked on the positive side, and the very next day, a trusted friend called me to talk about a huge opportunity that will allow me to help more athletes all over the country. Jackpot. You see, keeping positive attracts more positive things into your life, while staying negative attracts more negativity. Yes, I lost some money and time, but now I know better AND a huge window of opportunity just opened up. Major score!!!

So much of how we see our life and our surroundings does have to do with the people whom we choose to associate with. That's why those negative clients would not have been good in the long run anyway. But let's talk about how this can happen not just in our professional lives, but also in our social lives. As an example, in high school, I think a large part of my depression and low energy was in my nutrition, but also in the fact that I spent my time socially with people who felt that the world was against them. In retrospect, I feel that most of them also came from difficult family situations, which couldn't have been easy. I wasn't socially astute enough to understand that in high school. To me, they were just my friends and I didn't feel like I was accepted by my other peers or that anyone understood me. This led me to accept this idea that I was an outcast when really, I didn't need to be. When I look back on my experiences in high school, there was so much that I could have done to get along with other people my age, and yet I realize I often chose the opposite behavior. I would have a very different experience if I had to do high school again (no thank you, by the way). In college though, I went in with a totally different mindset. I was ready to try new things. I joined different clubs, I had new experiences. My friends in college came from all different demographics and those who did come from tough family situations were keenly aware of it and worked to bring themselves above it. I found amazing people to be friends with in college because I was ready for them. I brought up my energy levels and was then able to connect with other people operating on that level as well. So does it surprise me at all that basically all of my friends from college are currently superstars in their own personal lives? Not one bit. They are engineers, police officers, stay-at-home moms, teachers, authors, and more. They are happy, well-compensated for what they do, and, above all, still wonderful people. Why was I still low energy or even sometimes depressed in college? Bad sleep schedules, a terrible diet, a poor understanding of how caffeine affects me, and you know, I might have gone out drinking one or two nights (*hello*? Alcohol is a *depressant*). Even as a senior in college, I began to realize that having even one or two drinks really put me in a bad place the following day or two, which is why I really don't ever drink anymore. According to Dr. Amen, alcohol also kills all of the good bacteria in your gut, and YES, those little guys can greatly affect your mood and sense of well-being. Read up on it. It's a thing. This brings us to the next thing that can help with your energy and mood: your nutrition

Nutrition: If you were really malnourished, you would probably have really low energy all of the time, right? Unfortunately, in the United States, it is very easy to be overfed, overweight and *still* undernourished. So how is that possible? Processed foods have hardly any nutritional value, and so many of us practically live on that stuff. I know I did, and I could never really figure out why my weight was a constant struggle. In college and high school I would yoyo between 150 and 175 (crazy, because I don't even weigh that much with only a few weeks left in my pregnancy), and I really didn't have a clue as to why that would happen. Hence, I tried every diet out there and thought that I just couldn't consistently keep the weight off: that it was genetically impossible for me. Meanwhile, I was eating a lot of diner food, bagels, breads, and absolutely zero fats because I was under the impression that fats made you fat. So I was basically not eating ANYTHING with any nutritional value! Plus, I had no idea about food sensitivities and how they were precipitating my constant migranes. If I had only known all of this stuff back then!

So portion control is important for maintaining a good weight, but the most important thing for your enery is that you are avoiding the things that your body is reacting to and that you are eating for nutrient density. This simply means that you should stick to the foods that are the most chock full of vitamins and minerals and stay away from the empty calorie stuff. For example, a bagel with jelly (something I LOVED to eat lots of in college) has almost zero nutritional value, even though it has a ton of calories. Bowl of pasta? Ditto. That frozen dinner from the supermarket? Also crap. It has been really easy to manage my weight since becoming vegan because fruits and vegetables are some of the most nutrient dense things out there. Beans are excellent too. Being gluten free means that I am really always eating bread made of buckwheat, brown rice, or other nutrient-dense grains, which are way more filling and nutritious than white flour. Nuts and seeds: wow are they nutrient dense. Let me make this very simple for you. You don't have to go vegan (though it is one of the best decisions I have ever made in my life), but I do recommend your diet be composed mainly of the following:

-Organic fruits and vegetables
-Beans
-Nuts and seeds
-Nutrient dense grains and pseudograins (quinoa, millet, buckwheat, teff, wild rice, "forbidden" rice, etc.)
-Superfoods (like goji berries, moringa, maca, acai and so many more: all of these things are in shakeology, by the way)

I would strongly recommend that you avoid all dairy and also limit your intake of corn, since corn can interfere with the absorption of certain vitamins and minerals and dairy causes tremendous inflammation. All of those great vitamins and minerals affect how you function at a cellular level, so you will see your energy levels skyrocket after a few weeks of eating well.

Hydration: So much of your body is made out of water. Therefore, if you are not hydrated, things will not function as well. Your energy and mood can really suffer. Water is 75% of your brain, but that's just the start. Water helps to regulate your body temperature, decrease fatigue, prevent constipation, carry oxygen to your cells, flush toxins out, and so much more! For most people, 8 8 oz servings of water should be sufficient for one day. These needs might increase if it is extremely hot or you are working out a lot. Remember that not all beverages are created equal. Some beverages actually dehydrate you. If you think that drinking 8 8oz cups of coffee a day will replace the water, you will be sorely disappointed. Anything with caffeine in it will actually work to DEHYDRATE you, and this includes any "energy drinks." Although this may be surprising for many of you, it also includes some Vitamin Water and even Bai. Why? There are sneaky versions of caffeine in these drinks, which can make them even more nefarious.

What are some other sneaky things that might be dehydrating you?

-Too much protein can be dehydrating (another reason why you don't want to eat tons of protein right before hitting the gym or playing in a game).
-If your blood sugar gets very high, dehydration can also ensue. That's just one more reason to be mindful of your sugar intake.

Those are just a few simple things to be on the lookout for when it comes to hydration. Most people find that when they drink adequate amounts of water and avoid things that can be dehydrating their energy levels naturally increase.

Emotional well-being: Your energy levels and your emotional well-being are inextricably linked. If I told you right now that you just won a free trip to ANYWHERE in the world, you would probably jump up and down and have lots of energy, even if you were exhausted moments before. To foster emotional well-being, it really helps to see everything sunny side up (as we discussed earlier), it helps to be around people that support you (also discussed earlier), but it also helps to do a few more things:

1. **Dig through your own personal mess and deal with it**: this is a hard one for a lot of us to hear, but so much of where we fail in life is just based on subconscious scripts. This means that if you have heard that you are a wild zebra for most of your natural life, you will start believing that you are a wild zebra, and, let's face it, weird stuff is bound to happen. More realistically, maybe you have lots of subconscious scripts around weight loss. Most of the time genetics are not really a factor, it has more to do with the fact that you saw your mom struggle with weight and so you automatically assume that losing weight is hard work. Meanwhile, if other scripts were in place, weight loss wouldn't be so tough. I now realize that I was working off of some very odd subconscious scripts for a long time in my life. I had to really rewrite these scripts and do some soul-searching to take control of my life. I rectified much of this with Havening and hypnosis (why I decided to become certified in both disciplines), but I know that many people prefer talk therapy. Hey, whatever floats your boat. I'm just

pointing out that you are going to have a hard time moving forward if your subconscious is making a lot of bad decisions that you are basically unaware of. For a really in depth explanation of how all of this works, you can read *The Biology of Belief*, which I recommend you read anyway. You might find that you have a lot of self-sabotaging behaviors in areas that you struggle with.

2. **Make decisions**: This is really important. When you stay on the fence about lots of different things in life then you are going to be unhappy. Are you thinking about moving? Either do it or don't, but don't dream about why you should do it, and constantly talk about it, but still stay exactly where you are. Wanna quit your job? Really think about it, but either really make a commitment to stay and be great at what you do or leave and be great at something else. For goodness sake, though, stop half-assing things. As soon as you find yourself being more decisive, you will feel more in control of your life. This will improve your energy AND make you happier.

3. **Get over "trauma" quickly**: I know this sounds hard to hear, but dwelling on a loss or staying stuck on an event that you perceive to be traumatic is actually (at least in part) a choice. When I had my wrist injury in college, I realize now that I was choosing to act as a victim and feel sorry for myself and that made my recovery time extremely slow. It also made me really depressed. So, if your cat dies, I don't expect you to go dancing in the street or go out that very day and adopt a kitten. What I do suggest, however, is that you give yourself a period of time to get over it and then DECIDE to move on. This is what's best for everyone. Your cat would want you to move on. Unless your cat was a total bitch, in which case, good riddance.

Loving what you do: My first adult attempt at employment did not go as I had anticipated. My career choice as an English teacher seemed to make sense for me: I loved teaching and I loved literature. What didn't quite fit was the hours, the politics, and the fact that I was in high demand as a pitching coach as well. On paper, I should have loved my job, but I hated it. I felt like I would have preferred to be a professional shoe licker. If I taught high school English now, would it be better? Maybe. I probably won't ever find out, though, because *I really* love what I do. I have a dream job. I can't imagine NOT doing this. Even if I got a tremendous offer to go on and do something else, I can't picture my life without giving lessons or helping athletes find their dream colleges or helping people with health and nutrition. These are all things that I love and so my energy for them is renewed every day. If your source of income isn't something that you love doing and you can't find a way to make yourself enjoy it, then you are wasting a lot of your life in a very unhappy state. This is a huge drain on your energy every single day. I hate to even think about that! Before I get you too worked up, though, don't quit your job immediately. Instead, explore what you truly love and see if it is a viable source of income. You can even do that while working at the job that you don't love so much. Just realize that you will almost always have more energy when you are passionate about something. There are people who totally love learning about the stock market, or geek out over accounting, or love crochet. That's totally wonderful: with hard work and discipline, your passion in any of these areas can make you a profit!

Thyroid condition/other medical conditions: Finally, from an energy standpoint, if you have made some major lifestyle changes and your energy is still terrible, then you should probably get your thyroid checked by your doctor. I have known a few people over the years who have had difficulty with energy and/or weight loss and it turns out that they had thyroid issues all along. That is something that you need to address right away. Your doctor or pharmacist can go over some options once you have a diagnosis. The other thing that can really affect your energy levels is mental illness. Of all of the things that are still stigmatized in our society, I can't believe that mental illness is STILL stigmatized, but we need to start having some conversations about that. I have a few bipolar friends who are amazing people and do wonderful things. They are also amazing parents. They have worked with medical professionals to get the right treatments and they are inspirational in every way. Mental illness is something that doesn't have to hold you back, you just need to get help for it: the same way you would need to get help if you had diabetes (seriously!). Depression, borderline personality disorder, addiction, hoarding: look, these are all serious things and you shouldn't EVER have to be ashamed of them. Go seek a professional who can help you. It will change your life, your energy AND the lives of those around you.

7 KAIZEN

Ever since I can remember, I have been in awe of Japan. I have been fascinated by its culture, its landscape, its technology, and so much more. So about two years ago, I finally told my husband that we were going to go to Japan. I was really excited, but also scared. Japan is very far and I really dislike long plane rides. I also recognize it as one of the most seismically active places on the planet, and that was a little scary too.

The more I read about Japan prior to our visit, however, the more I wanted to do. My only regret in visiting Japan is that I really should have scheduled a longer trip.

If you aren't at all familiar with Japan, you would probably be amazed at how they have created trains that go hundreds of miles an hour. You would also be amazed at how friendly everyone is and how very safe it is basically everywhere. You wouldn't really be anxious to walk around at night in any neighborhood. They also have a tremendous infrastructure meant to withstand the constant seismic activity in that area. The accomplishments of the Japanese really blew me away. As I became more and more familiarized with their culture, I realized that there were two components that really made this possible:

Kaizen: What this idea means is that you work to get just a little better every single day. It is not just a concept, but a well-practiced value in Japan. If you are working on making trains, then you strive just to get a little better at that practice every day. This is how, over years and years, Japan has become incredibly advanced technologically. It is also why, despite the challenges of creating infrastructure in a very seismically active area, Japan has created an infrastructure that basically puts ours to shame. If you have ever had to deal with the expense and terrible lateness of Amtrak, and then you have ridden the shinkansen, you will think that you have died and gone to heaven. These trains run on time (to the second) and take you across the country in almost no time. They are also very safe and very comfortable.

Meiwaku: The other principal that the Japanese live by is meiwaku. The best way I can describe it is something to the effect of "don't be annoying to other people" or "don't do things to other people that you wouldn't want them to do to you." This seems like common sense, but it isn't always common practice. In Japan, millions of people go in and out of Shinjiku station (which is immaculate, by the way) every day and there is nary a hitch. People do not run into each other. There is no homeless population, people do not yell at each other like they do in NYC stations and subways. At first, it feels like you have just entered some amazing parallel universe. Then you realize that that is just how people there are. I know an amazing coach who spent a lot of time playing and coaching over there and she explained it this way: if you are playing baseball or softball in America and you are pitching, when your teammate makes an error, it might feel natural to blame them or to get upset with them. In Japan, if you are pitching and your teammate makes an error, you might think something like, "how can I pitch the ball better the next time so that it won't be so hard for her to field?" This thinking might seem really bizarre to us as Americans, but you can probably see where it can make for better relationships and allow for others to be more understanding of one another. If we always stopped for a second and thought about the other person instead of immediately thinking about ourselves, we could avoid a lot of arguments, build stronger families, and feel more connected with others.

But then, we also have to be a little realistic. I mean, we aren't Japanese, so, as much as we might want to apply all of these awesome practices to our lives, we might also feel like outcasts if we do it too much in our American culture. So what are some ways that we can use these concepts to enhance our lives without being totally overwhelmed?

It's pretty simple, actually. The concept of kaizen is so much easier to apply than the idea of binging on one project. For example, with people who are trying to lose weight, they often try to do a new workout regimen, start a new diet, and then cut out every "bad" food that they ever loved all at once. If you just applied the concept of trying to get a little better every day, on the first day of your transformation, you might say something like, "today, I will not eat any processed foods." The next day, you might say, "I will not eat any processed foods and I will go for a walk." You don't need to beat yourself up over that cookie if you know that you are just trying to get a little better every day. Then eventually, one day you might not even want that cookie, because you are training yourself slowly and methodically to become more disciplined and to make better choices.

In the world of finances, you can probably see where something like this would have a huge impact. If you took $1 a day and put it in an index fund that kept reinvesting the dividends, you would make lots of money. Most people don't think that way, though. I mean, I get it: you want to get lots of money all at once. But people who have made lots of money understand exactly how many years are involved in creating a good business, financial security, and more. These things never happen overnight. And, though we might be impatient to get to the finish line, we can really only reach it by taking it one step at a time.

The concepts of Kaizen and meiwaku both have a strong place in the realm of relationships. I think that, for a long time, I thought that relationships were about how the other person made you feel and what the other person did for you. As I have matured, I realize that so much of creating a healthy relationship really means that you naturally WANT to do nice things for the other person and that you have found a way not only to work out your differences, but also to genuinely make each other happier. Here are some little ways to do that:

- Make your spouse some food for a day when you know they will be running around and won't have a chance to get something healthy
- Write a silly note or text somewhere that you know they will see it so that he or she knows you were thinking about them
- Put slippers and a towel by the door for him or her if you know they will be coming home on a day that is rainy or cold.
- Clean the house or take out the trash without being asked
- Post something nice on his or her social media (like on their Facebook timeline) so that he or she understands what you love about the person they are. This one totally gets me. I love it when I see people post really positive things on social media about their spouses, children, or friends. This also makes us grateful for what we have. The more we extoll the virtues of our loved ones and stop focusing on the negative, the more grateful we are for what they contribute to our lives.
- Focus on what you have in common instead of the things that drive you apart. Remember my awesome neighbors who are very involved in their church and their children and work together to make an amazing life? I am sure that there are some things that they don't share the same view on. Everyone is a little different. Instead, though, they choose to focus on the things that they do have in common, and they use those things to enrich their lives and the lives of those around them. People are just better for knowing them. As another example, my husband and I do share a lot of common ground. For example, we have a near-identical sense of humor (read: toilet humor and jokes that we stole from late-night cartoons), think that openly displaying affection is a good thing, and believe that the education system needs a huge revamping. We have also both been vegan for nearly a decade. On the other hand, many people would probably be really surprised to know that our views on religion and money vary pretty dramatically. If we focused on that sort of thing all of the time, it would create a really miserable marriage.
- Give compliments freely and with sincerity. Okay, if my husband is getting ready to leave the house with some fugly clothes on or he needs a shave, I am NOT going to tell him

that he looks amazing. I am just the world's worst liar and I definitely wouldn't' lie to him, even if it were to spare his feelings. He does have great taste in cologne, though, and so at the very least, I can almost always say, "you smell amazing." Frank is always quick to compliment me, even though I am now very pregnant and often wake up with what I jokingly refer to as "smudge face" (essentially a nice way of saying that my face was smashed by the pillow and my hair is a mess and standing up in forty different directions). Regardless, this morning when I woke up, he said "you look so beautiful," and he really meant it with sincerity. And I was so extremely grateful because no one feels pretty when they are super pregnant and then waddle out of bed in the morning. "Beautiful" is not usually on the list of descriptive words or phrases I would use. It would probably be more accurate to say, "you look like a manatee," or "you look ready to pop!" Therefore, getting such a great compliment completely made my day.

So I want you to notice something. None of the things that I have mentioned require any great expenditure of money. None of them really even require you to do very much, other than just be thoughtful and kind. So you will find that, by doing a few tiny things each day, your relationships will get stronger and stronger.

Finally, I think that meiwaku has applicability in almost all areas of life. You can just do simple things that are considerate, like avoiding playing loud music at midnight in your apartment with the very thin walls. You will also avoid being deceitful, because that is something that can really hurt others down the road. I also think that it a really good way to help with the spending of your money. You can spend your money getting loaded and having your friends baby sit you and constantly worry about you (which is very selfish), or you can spend your money going out to a play or ice skating or doing something that you can all enjoy. It's pretty simple. You don't have to overhaul your entire life. You just need to make some small changes that can really help you and help others. See? Now everyone is happy.

Julianne Soviero

8 GRATITUDE

You may or may not believe it, but this one little word is one of the biggest indicators of how happy you will be.

Yup.

So you may think, "if I only had $100,000, I would be happy" or "if I could only lose 10 pounds, I would be happy," or "if my husband was more affectionate, I would be happy."

The truth is, that happiness is a choice that a lot of us unwittingly make (or don't make), and a large portion of that choice has to do with gratitude.

If you consider the above statements and modify your perception of those circumstances to work happily with what you have, you will draw more positivity into your life. So instead of thinking of your finances as a source of worry or unhappiness, you can be grateful for the fact that you have some money in savings, you are paying down your debts, and you have some money in retirement accounts. You can then focus on other ways to make your money grow instead of just stressing out about it! If all of your energy goes to stressing out about money, it will simply create *more* stress around money and you won't feel like you are getting anywhere. If instead you are grateful for what you already have, you can focus on growing it or managing it better in general. If you focus on how your weight is causing you to be unhappy, and you create a victim mentality, you are going to be stuck exactly where you are at for a very long time. Many people will blame genetics for their weight or blame their jobs. You can either make excuses or make progress, but you can't make both. Instead of adopting a victim mentality, you can think about how nourished you feel every single time you eat healthfully, and how poorly you feel when you don't eat well. I have even heard of people who essentially show gratitude for the food at every level. For example, they are thankful to the tree that produced the orange and the tree that produced the nuts. If you find that your only gratitude from a food standpoint would go towards the factory workers who mass-produced those coco puffs or to the slaughter house where that bacon came from, you should also show gratitude that you don't yet have diabetes or the other health problems associated with eating like shit. I'm just being honest. Look at your food and the fact that you even *can* eat with great love and gratitude. There are so many people in this world who are just not able to even have the opportunity to eat. So many people are literally starving. On the other hand, if you find yourself saying things like, "I am grateful to this genetically modified cow that has been pumped full of hormones and antibiotics and has had her babies stolen from her so that I can enjoy this yogurt," then karmically that might not be so great for you. Also, dairy can make it very hard to keep inflammation down and lose weight, as you already know. Finally, instead of wishing that your husband was more affectionate, do some nice things for him, or have a gentle talk with him telling him that you would like him to be more affectionate. He can't read your mind. Some people feel weird about PDAS and he might just want to be cuddly in private. Maybe he is just not communicating that. Or maybe he likes to show affection in different ways, that you don't really understand yet. Listen. Be patient. People cannot, as of yet, communicate through telepathy, so there are still going to be times when we communicate poorly: even with the people who are closest to us. You generally can't go wrong if you express love and joy, though. You will also find that if you are always thankful for your husband's best attributes, you will fall in love with him even more deeply and will be more forgiving of what you perceive his faults to be. Every day, think about the things that made you fall in love with him to begin with, and allow those feelings to blossom and allow you to see other amazing things that he does.

So you might look at my analyses of the above scenarios and think, "well she is just farting out sunshine and probably was born that way. She has probably never been sad." That, my friends, is a bunch of mythical hogwash. When I was younger, I had several intense periods of depression, and was even on antidepressants for quite a while.

I sympathize with you. I have been where you are. I have trained myself to be happy: and not in a cultish, "look who drank the Kool-aid" sort of way. It has literally been years and years of very hard work.

I can give you a little background. See if any of this resonates with you.

I remember, at about 12 years old, my family and I first moved from our original home in Commack. In Commack, I had two friends around the block, got some of the best grades in my class, and generally loved my environment. We moved out to a big house that was very far from our neighbors. It was a very lonely summer, but I thought that maybe the school year would bring some new friends. It didn't. And as weeks of loneliness turned into months, I became very depressed. To the point where I was wondering why I should even continue living.

This is a very hard thing to write, also because mental illness and depression are very stigmatized (still), which is completely ridiculous, and I think it is something that stops a lot of people from getting the help that they need.

I remember when my parents and I finally spoke about it, though, they were so baffled. In their eyes, didn't we just move to a better school district? A bigger, new house? What about people who had *real* problems, they wondered. So many people were starving in Africa when we had so much. Why was I having trouble seeing that?

In my dad's defense, he is the type of person who will take some time alone in church every week and thank God for all of the wonderful things in his life. He did this even when he had cancer. He did this even when his parents were infirm and dying. He did this even when, from an outsider's standpoint, it would look like there wasn't a whole lot to be happy about. So, you know, hearing that his young daughter was depressed while living in this big house that he had spent years dreaming about just probably made no sense at all to him. If I had to do it all over again, I definitely would have taken some time to look at the more positive aspects of the move, be grateful for them, and use them as a catalyst to draw MORE positivity into my life. Instead, I went to therapy, and chose friends among the people who were sort of social outcasts. But when they started doing drugs and drinking, I even became isolated from them, since there was no way that I was going to do drugs. Hence, I spent my whole middle school and high school career in various states of depression.

A large part of coming out of depression was meeting my husband during my senior year in college. I only dated two others prior to him, but my husband was very different. He would sometimes drive home behind me to make sure that I got home safely. He would throw amazing compliments at me and tell me how I wasn't like anyone he had ever known. He brought a kind of love into my life that I didn't know was possible. Then I started to slowly come off of the antidepressants. I started to get ambitious. I started thinking outside of the box because he thinks outside of the box. He challenges the status quo, and that can be frustrating at times, but it is also a way to see things from a different perspective. When I was miserable at work, he encouraged me to quit the job that I hated and start my own business. He has always believed in me. He has always encouraged me. He has also always been fiercely protective of me, so that I know I am not in danger when I am around him. Because Frank allowed me to challenge my thinking, I learned about how eating affected depression. I got into Havening and hypnosis. I also learned that the more purpose I have, the happier I am. So I am incredibly grateful to him. I am also extremely grateful to Vito LaFata and Rob Crews: two mentors who have always encouraged me to work on personal development and be the very best I can be. It's hard to be sad when you are constantly trying to make yourself better. Then, even if you are sad for a minute, you know that things are going to change as you constantly work to improve your life.

Another thing that can really help you if you are mentally down in the dumps is volunteering or giving money to charity. People who volunteer their time and give to charity also tend to be better off financially than their counterparts who don't engage in those behaviors. I know it sounds strange, but this is directly from page 189 in the book *The Thin Green Line*: "'People who give to charity are forty-three percent more likely than people who don't give to say they're very happy people,' said Arthur Brooks, president of the American Enterprise Institute. 'People who give blood are twice as likely to say they're very happy people as people who don't give blood. People who volunteer are happier. The list goes on . You simply can't find any kind of service that won't make you happier.'"

Right now, write down some things that you are grateful for (it might even help you to think of some things that annoy you, and then turn those things around to be grateful for them, just as I did in the examples above. Beneath that, think of some charities you would like to support, either with your money or your time, and then you are working your way towards a happier life in just a few steps.:

Things I am grateful for:

1.
2.
3.
4.
5.

Charities that I would like to volunteer for or donate money to:
1.
2.
3.

9 MOTIVATION

Motivation is a funny thing, and I suspect it is somewhat bipolar. One minute, motivation is right in front of your face jumping on a trampoline with a bull horn and insisting that you get off your ass and start making things happen! So you start to listen. Maybe you take the first steps. You buy that fitness program. You start writing a book. You begin saving money. Then when you look for motivation to help you out again, he is in the corner sleeping and farting loudly and simply cannot be bothered to give you that great cheerleading segment that he gave you before.

I mean, the nerve.

Let's talk like real human beings for a minute. There are going to be days when you feel motivated enough to clean your whole house, master trapeze, and wrestle that alligator next door. On the other hand, there are going to be days when you are barely motivated enough to find a new show to binge watch on Hulu. So what can we do to kind of even things out a little?

If you go back to the concept of Kaizen, you will find that, just by doing a little every day, you will see progress, which can be very motivating in and of itself. That is simply not enough for a lot of people though. This is where it gets really important to ask yourself the following question:

WHY?

Those three letters are very powerful. Without addressing them, you can't really begin to expect success on any level. If you don't have a strong WHY, you will find that you come up with a million reasons for WHY NOT, and then your goals turn to shit really quickly.

For example, if you begin a workout regimen and eating plan because you want to lose weight, that is usually not enough for most people to succeed. EVERYONE wants to lose weight.

So let's take a different scenario. Let's say that you go to the doctor and the doctor says that if you don't get your shit together healthwise that you won't be around another 5 years.

I mean, who is going to be more motivated?

The other thing that seems to motivate people tremendously about losing weight is if they are somehow really embarrassed by it. For example, if someone thought that a woman was pregnant when she was just heavy, or maybe a man tried to go for a walk with a friend and couldn't even make it around the block.

Do you think that you would be more concerned about your health and wellness then?

In all likelihood, yes.

So the thing is, that if you really want to achieve your goals, your WHY always has to be stronger than your excuses, and then you need to build habits around your WHY every day.

I always have so many goals, but, for the most part, I haven't created good road maps for achieving them. Ever since I had several Spanish-speaking friends in college, I have been saying how I really want to learn Spanish. In an attempt to learn, I would end up getting these Spanish CDs and listening to them in the car. Here's the problem: I would do it sporadically. I would really increase my vocabulary that way, but my grammar and my ability to do conjugations was a nightmare. I got to this point where, as long as you spoke slowly and simply, I could understand you, but I couldn't respond at all (except to ask you to slow down if you were speaking too quickly). This was frustrating and I started asking everyone who spoke Spanish what the best way to learn was. I got a bunch of different answers that didn't work for me, but then I asked a Spanish teacher. She recommended an app that sends me notifications to practice every single day. This app ensures that I don't just passively listen, but I have to write out sentences and do conjugations and work on possession. The fifteen minutes I do every morning has been amazing. Now I can practice with my husband, and I progress every few weeks. For over a decade, I wanted to do it, but didn't make my road map. Just like in real life, without a map or a GPS, your best intentions will only lead you so far. In order for your motivation to be successful, you are going to need a game plan that is doable for YOU. Not the thing that works for your neighbor, but the thing that works for you.

Using fitness as an example again, I feel like so many people wait so long to hire a personal trainer or join an online community or to start a reasonable eating program because they feel that they can figure it out themselves. The thing is, though, how many weeks and months are you going to waste figuring it out for yourself? As far as my business is concerned, I would still be struggling to figure things out YEARS after starting. That simply doesn't make sense. Instead, my friend Deanna has guided me tremendously and then I hired people to help me in other areas. These are people who have saved me enormous amounts of time and effort by sharing their own expertise with me. I knew I needed to hire a business coach at some point because I love what I do, but don't have a background in business and am still learning so much (even after about 12 years of being in business: crazy). Imagine if I had just asked a Spanish teacher for help when I originally wanted to commit myself to learning Spanish. I would have literally been fluent by now.

I am sure that you can think of similar mistakes that you have made in your own life: when you were motivated enough to set out to achieve a goal on your own, but not EDUCATED enough to accomplish it on your own. I think that a lot of people make this mistake with their finances. This is how a lot of people end up way over their heads with debt and other financial woes. With financial goals (like "I want to retire by the time I am 60") you REALLY need a roadmap because with that, even $5 a day can actually make or break you. David Bach calls this "the latte effect" and it essentially boils down to the fact that, if you use the $5 you spend on coffee every day to pay down your debts or invest, you would be in very good financial standing. I love his financial advice and highly recommend his books. But in his example (with buying a coffee outside your home every day), you are LITERALLY PEEING OUT about $150 a month or $1800 a year. Doh! That means, that if you had some serious financial goals and you started those goals ten years ago, you could have about $18000 to put towards them. Like seriously!!!! I know. Don't beat yourself up about it. Make it simple instead, and just address these questions:

What are my top 3 goals in life right now?
1.
2.
3.

WHY do I NEED to achieve these goals? In other words, what is your motivation that will NOT fizzle out over time? What means THAT much to you?

1.
2.
3.

Who will support me in achieving these goals (hello success partner or accountability partner)?
1.
2.
3.

What is my daily habit or habits that will help me achieve these goals?
1.
2.
3.
4.

Okay, so we didn't talk too much about the last one. We just kind of insinuated some stuff. But let's talk about some examples.

If I want to be in the best shape of my life, my daily habit has to be working out and using the portion control containers 6 days a week.

If I want to speak Spanish fluently in two years, I have to do 15 minutes of Spanish every morning and then practice with my husband at night (even if we just make up silly phrases like "your elephant drinks milk").

If I want to grow the reach of my business, I have to post on social media daily, write a blog weekly, and get involved in some coaching groups.

The nice thing about all of this stuff is that it doesn't take MASSIVE amounts of motivation. You can very easily fit stuff like this into your schedule instead of doing stuff that is a waste of your time. If you have developed habits, and you always keep your WHY in mind, then you really don't have to worry much about whether or not you will achieve your goals, because it all adds up.

So for my daily habits, I do the following:
15 minutes or more of Spanish at breakfast
Workout immediately after breakfast.
Work on business building and expanding my reach during lunch.
Spend 1-3 hours either writing or working on Beachbody business
Work with clients until 9 every night.
Relax with hubby for an hour or so
Go to bed

I make it a point to read at least one thing every day that helps with financial planning or budgeting or removing debt etc. I also spend at least one day a week paying bills and taking my financial stats, as it were, to keep everything in order.

See? That's not so bad. I can assure you that I mostly have a very nice schedule. I see between 12 and 20 clients on some days, but I have help for that, and I can almost ALWAYS fit my daily habits in. If I can't, then I reevaluate. Why was that important to me again? If it isn't important anymore, I trade it up for a new habit.

The other thing that I do if I am really having trouble being motivated, is I will make a little reward for myself. So after I finish this chapter, I get to use an Amazon gift card!!! Yay Amazon. I try not to make the rewards related to food, though, since that can be dangerous for your waistline. Maybe your reward is a massage or a walk. Maybe it's a phone call to a friend. Maybe it's fifteen minutes of reading a really trashy book. Hey, these all work. Don't judge yourself. As long as you aren't hurting anyone, using food as reward, or spending exorbitant amounts of money in the process, rewards are a great motivator.

10 YOUR COMFORT ZONE AND WHY IT SUCKS

You may have heard the following expression before: "the comfort zone is a beautiful place, but nothing grows there."

When I was doing 80 Day Obsession the other day, Autumn Calabrese said that exact statement, and then one of the individuals she was training said, "my love handles grew in the comfort zone."

This made me laugh really hard, but it also made me realize that we should probably adjust that phrase a little: "the comfort zone is a beautiful place, but nothing GOOD grows there." Basically, everything that I have ever done that has taken me out of my comfort zone has changed my life in a positive way. Going to Japan was something that I always wanted to do, but was way outside of my comfort zone. Coaching in Italy when my Italian was mensa mensa (at best) was totally out of my comfort zone. Learning how to manage finances like an adult and set myself up for life was sooooo out of my comfort zone. Yet I can't imagine my life without having done these amazing things. Another thing that has been really out of my comfort zone was learning to talk to my husband about money. For those of you who don't know, money is basically the number one cause of divorce in the US. I can understand why. We used to fight about it a ton. We still do, BUT we have learned how to communicate better about it. So much of improving our communication began with me reading different books on finance and then passing them off to my husband and talking about how we could apply some of the ideas in the books to our lives. This might be a good starting point for you too if discussing finances with your spouse sounds worse than having to vomit through your nose.

Wanna know what else was way out of my comfort zone? Getting pregnant. I have definitely had some disordered eating in the past, and I was afraid of all of that weight gain and that my body might change permanently. That was one of the many reasons why I wanted to adopt. But now that I feel this beautiful little soul moving around inside me every day and calming me when I am upset, I am incredulous that I almost didn't do this!!!! I can't describe the love I feel for this little baby, who was so out of my comfort zone, but worth stretching it in every way.

Here's the thing, though. If you are afraid of heights, you probably don't want to go bungee jumping right away. I know that, with me and pregnancy, I had to do a lot of Havening and a lot of personal development to get where I am today. I had to challenge some long-held beliefs of mine. My husband and I were foster parents to two beautiful boys for a long time, and, after learning that we could not adopt them (and feeling totally destroyed by this news for weeks and weeks), I still came away knowing that my husband and I were able to parent two boys who had been through some really difficult times: I knew that I *could* be a parent, even if I couldn't be a permanent parent to those boys.

The way that I managed to get over to Japan, even though that was way out of my comfort zone, was that we stopped in Canada for a few days on the way, which allowed us to break up the flight. Now that I have done it once, I realize that I could have really done the flight with one stopover (which is what we did on the way back) with no problem, but I needed to take those baby steps to get out of my comfort zone in general.

Some other things that I have done that took me outside of my comfort zone:
Public speaking
Buying a house
Traveling by myself
Starting my own business

The list goes on, but all of these things have been amazing for me in the end, and I think that, if I just led a comfortable life and never

ever pushed I would probably still be miserable teaching high school English.

Why?

If you don't do the hard stuff, you will always fear the worst about the hard stuff. Living your life in fear is definitely no way to go. You have the opportunity every day to go out and seize the best things that life has to offer. But let's be honest: sometimes we are scared. Sometimes other people tell us that we can't. Sometimes the issues of the past hold us back (if so, try Havening, hypnosis, or therapy).

How can you start leaving your comfort zone and making strides towards your dreams? First, make a list of all of the things that you have wanted to do but haven't done because they made you feel uncomfortable. These can be small things like maybe going on a rollercoaster with your kids. They can also be huge things like starting your own business doing something that you love. Maybe you want to take a huge financial leap like buying a house (if so, I strongly recommend that you read *Your Money or Your Life* first) or making an investment in index funds. Regardless, write them down and realize that you can't tackle all of them at once. Decide either which are the most important to you OR which ones come with an expiration date. Realize that there are some things that you will never be able to do again once the window of opportunity passes (either biologically or because of other extenuating circumstances.) Just be sure to go after these first, since you don't want to spend your whole like wondering, "what if?"

Things I want to do that are outside of my comfort zone

1.
2.
3.
4.
5.

Beneath that, write about WHY each of those things is out of your comfort zone. Did you have a particular experience that was bad and soured you on the idea of doing anything new? Do you have issues with anxiety in general? Have you always heard, "you shouldn't do that," from other people, and it started to stick? You might need a little time to figure out why you struggle to do certain things that are easy for other people. Just remember that sometimes a little education can save you a lot of stress.

Why these things are outside of my comfort zone

1.
2.
3.
4.
5.

Now think about some small things that you can do that will gradually allow you to break free of that comfort zone and accomplish your dreams. So, for example, let's say that one of the things that I want to do that is out of my comfort zone is speaking to groups about the importance of health and wellness. I realize that this is out of my comfort zone because, when I was younger, I had to do presentations in high school that I was often ill-prepared for (and therefore didn't go well). So now, some baby steps I can take to rectify this are
1. Take a class (or classes) on speaking: there are some really good ones out there.
2. Research and prepare something that will suit my audience
3. Practice in front of family and friends ONLY initially
4. Set up a SMALL group of people to speak in front of

From there, you can get more ambitious. You can do more and more. I personally find that if you determine the cause of your trepidation, things go so much more smoothly. You can also just go straight for hypnosis or Havening. I once worked with a Math teacher who was an absolutely amazing teacher and person, but was very nervous about giving a presentation in front of other teachers. She was so passionate about her profession and just so amazing in general. For these reasons, I couldn't imagine that this woman would ever give a bad presentation, but she did have some fear and trepidation in that area. So I hypnotized her, and afterwards I remember her telling me about how she felt like a different person during her presentation: how she stood up on the desk and came out of her shell (she was more of a shy, quiet type). As you can imagine, I was over the moon with joy and she was so glad that she did the hypnosis. Even going for hypnosis might be out of the comfort zone for some people, though. That's okay! Start small, but start SOMEWHERE and do a little bit every day (kaizen!).

I wanted to close this book with the chapter on your comfort zone because oftentimes we don't feel as though it is something that holds us back. We are, by definition, comfortable, so we don't want to really change anything. That also makes it hard for us to grow as people, though, which is why I would strongly suggest doing at least a little bit of personal development every day. You will see where, no matter what age you are, you are able to stretch, grow, and expand your limits. This is my greatest hope for you with this entire book. It is nice to be wealthy, and fit, and to have great relationships, BUT you have to start by having the right relationship with yourself. Understand more about yourself and what you can do to become better not *just* for yourself, but for others as well. This will change your life in ways that would be hard for you to imagine. Never stop questioning . Never stop building. Never stop growing. Never stop loving. Never stop dreaming. Never stop making a positive impact on the world.

ABOUT THE AUTHOR

Julianne Soviero is a speaker, writer, coach, and personal development addict. She wrote this particular book (her third) because she felt that more people need short, quick bursts of personal development that are easy to apply. You can contact Julianne for speaking or coaching at Juliannesoviero@gmail.com.

Printed in the USA
CPSIA information can be obtained
at www.ICGtesting.com
LVHW020920070124
768343LV00010B/674